Geek Speak Magazine
Presents

THE BEST OF
B. C. ROBERTS

From the pages of
Geek Speak Magazine

Overlord Publishing
overlordpublishing.com

For Bradley.

CONTENTS

INTRODUCTION

When the grand adventure that eventually became *Geek Speak Magazine* was but a glimmer in the internet's eye, one of the first intrepid souls to sign on was the inimitable B. C. Roberts. With a mind as sharp as his wit, and a penchant for extreme views on some of our beloved genre's more left-field offerings, along with a very solid grounding in its many stalwarts (even despite suffering from an inexplicable disinterest in *Star Trek*), he was a natural fit for a spiritual home at which it was not only perfectly acceptable but actively encouraged to declaim a passionate devotion to the genius of *Underworld*.

From our first issue in early-2010 to our very last post in late-2017, B. C. was with us, fighting the good fight (or the morally dubious but still very well-argued fight) and delighting us all with his uniquely cynical yet enthusiastic view of all things genre. From his love of *Balls of Fury* to his hatred of fan service, and from his love of Harry Potter to his disgust with comic crossover continuity, he kept us guessing, and chuckling, as he frankly, often harshly, but never rashly took aim at whatever was particularly annoying him – or pleasing him – that day/week/month/year/lifetime.

Even if he did turn everything in late.

Here, collected for the first time are his most memorable moments from seven years of geek speaking. I'd say "enjoy," but honestly, there is no need. Of course you will.

– Rachel Hyland, Editor-in-Chief
Melbourne, 2018

REVIEWS
FILM

Back to the Future Part II (1989)

Story by: Robert Zemeckis and Bob Gale
Written by: Bob Gale
Starring: Michael J Fox, Christopher Lloyd, Elisabeth Shue, Thomas F Wilson, Lea Thompson

Movie Marathon Category: Sequels

In Short: You've already seen it.
Recommended: Yes.

> **DOC BROWN:** The time-traveling is just too dangerous. Better that I devote myself to study the other great mystery of the universe: women

Let's be honest. You have already seen *Back to the Future Part II* and you think it's the worst of the trilogy. *[Oh, hey now! – Ed.]* It doesn't have the novelty of the first movie and it doesn't have the awesome Wild West setting of the third. It doesn't even have the coolest skateboarding scene in the trilogy, despite there being hoverboards. But it does have the single best line in any of the movies:

> **MARTY:** Hey Doc, you better back up we don't have enough road to get up to 88.
> **DOC:** Roads? Where we're going, we don't need *[melodramatic flick of futuristic sunglasses]* roads.

Back to the Future belongs in the category of family friendly sci-fi (or FFSF as I like to call it) and follows the adventures of Marty McFly (Michael J Fox) and Doctor Emmett Brown (Christopher Lloyd) as they bumble through time. And I do mean bumble. Despite having a time machine, our dynamic duo are never in control. This is normally the result of the peculiar requirements to get the time machine running: the flux capacitor (don't ask) needs 1.21 gigawatts – pronounced, by Doc Brown, "jigawatts" – of electricity and the DeLorean which houses the flux capacitor must be travelling at 88 miles per hour (142 kilometers per hour for us metric types). So in the first movie it's the lack of gigawatts which causes the problem (only solved with a handily placed lightning strike) and in the third movie it's the 88 miles per hour when the DeLorean runs out of petrol in the Wild West (solved in a quite fantastic train sequence).

But the second movie follows a different course. Doc and Marty travel from present to future to alternate present to past to present volitionally. They are still somewhat bumbling around – the purpose of their second and subsequent jumps is to put right mistakes made while they're in the future.

Hm, that sounds confusing. Why don't I explain? *Back to the Future II* starts with all the crap things in Marty's life still being fixed from his good work in the first movie. Luckier still for him is that his girlfriend has gotten an upgrade in the break between films to the delightful Elisabeth Shue (whom everyone should remember as the unlikely genius physicist opposite Val Kilmer in *The Saint*). They're about to head off for some much needed time alone when Doc appears out of nowhere in his time machine saying they need to go to the future to stop their kids from ending up in jail. Naturally. While in the future, Marty buys a sports almanac with all the sporting results from 1950 to 2000, with the idea of gambling his way to a life filled with expensive hookers and top-notch blow. Doc talks him out of it, they throw the almanac away, another character – that damnable bully, Biff (Thomas F. Wilson) – gets it, goes back to the past to give it to his old self and the old self gets super-rich, killing Marty's dad and marrying his Mom in the process. This is obviously a situation that no self-respecting time traveler can endure, so Marty and Doc set about fixing it.

I'm not sure that clarified anything. See the point is that this movie is even more convoluted than your average time travelling tale, though it does make slightly more sense than any of the *Austin Powers* movies. Where the other *Back to the Future* movies spend most of the movie in one era, *Part II* jumps repeatedly through time and loses in the process all the signature anachronisms, like Marty's mother trying to kiss him in 1955 or Doc creating a house-sized contraption just to make an ice-cube in 1855.

So *Part II* is really the action movie of the trilogy; it moves quickly from time to time with no slowdown. The others are more languid and evoke a much stronger sense of place and time despite, or maybe because, they don't show quite so many times and places. *Part II* is a great and necessary part of the trilogy (three identically-styled movies would be tedious) which makes it a must-watch but when you're looking for a fix of the best *Back to the Future* action, stick to the others.

– B. C. Roberts, 2010

-:--:--:--:--:- *GS* -:--:--:--:--:-

Balls of Fury (2007)

Written by: Tom Lennon and Robert Ben Garant
Directed by: Robert Ben Garant
Starring: Dan Fogler, George Lopez, Christopher Walken, James Hong and Maggie Q

Movie Marathon Category: Sports

In Short: I love it. You might too.
Recommended: Hells Yes.

> **MASTER WONG:** Ping Pong is not the Macarena. It takes patience. She is like a fine, well-aged prostitute... it takes years to learn her tricks. She is cruel, laughs at you when you are naked, but you keep coming back for more, and more! Why? Because she is the only prostitute I can afford.

In this magazine I have defended many an unloved movie. From *DOA* to *Underworld*, it's clear that maybe I don't have the most high-brow taste in genre flicks. I don't love *2001*, can't really stand *Star*

Trek, and I've never (gasp) read the *Game of Thrones* books. My credentials aren't that solid.

But forget all that, because *Balls of Fury* is totally awesome.

And I don't mean so bad it's good, or so bad it's bad it's good. But rather that it's just straight out freakin' spectacular.

You heard me.

Balls of Fury is the story of Randy Daytona (Dan Fogler) who, as a 12-year-old, makes it to the table tennis final of the 1988 Olympics. He loses on the first point (by knocking himself out chasing a smash) and his father, who bet on the game, loses his life. Like all good kung fu/table tennis prodigies, Randy swears never to play competition table tennis again.

Years later, Randy is doing table tennis shows at a casino in Reno, playing to a bored audience more intent on eating their buffet meals than watching a guy in a blindfold hitting five ping pong balls. Unappreciated by the crowd Randy starts bouncing the ball off the head of some poor chump going back to the buffet. The poor guy starts complaining (I just want some more cheese and mac) and then crying before having a heart attack. Randy gets fired.

It's all going well so far.

Better, since Randy's assistant is a 60-year-old woman dressed up in feathers:

> **RANDY:** Thank you, Bethany
> **SARAH:** My name's Sarah
> **RANDY:** Really?
> **SARAH:** You've called me that name for the last five years... but that's fine.

From there we are introduced to FBI agent Ernie Rodriguez (George Lopez). Though Randy is worried that he's in trouble for almost killing the audience member Rodriguez tells him "That's not why I'm here. Actually I thought that was part of the show. Until the paramedics showed up I was laughing my ass off."

Hilarious.

Rodriguez needs Randy's unique skills to get him to an *Enter the Dragon* style ping pong tournament held by the generally nefarious Feng (Christopher Walken – the details of his criminal enterprise are irrelevant). Feng is, of course, the man responsible for the death of Randy's father.

Randy trains with Feng's old master, the blind Master Wong (James Hong), falls in love with Wong's niece (the super- super-*super*-hot Maggie Q) and gets into the tournament after defeating the fiercely named Dragon. At the tournament Randy discovers matches are to the death with losers eliminated by blow dart from the beautiful Mahogany (Aisha Tyler pretending she's an Amazon). With no way to escape Randy plays his way through the field to the final against the same man who eliminated him from the 1988 Olympics, the nasty East German Karl Wolfschtagg (Thomas Lennon), a man whose trash talking knows no depths of shame.

> **KARL:** I'm sorry your daddy isn't here to see you today. I think he would be very proud of you. So proud of you he would probably bet some money on you. I could use the cash. Haha.

After an inspiring speech by Master Wong ("game not in paddle, game in you") Randy faces Wolfschtagg confidently, only to have him replaced by Maggie in a weird twist that doesn't make a huge amount of sense but provides the best line of the movie: "I'm trying to sacrifice my life for our love Randy. Stop being such a dick."

What is beautiful about *Balls of Fury* is that it takes a great kung fu movie like *Enter the Dragon*, which is so iconic as to have become a complete cliché, and with a completely straight face remakes it as a movie about ping pong. There's no laughing to the camera about how absurd the premise is – which is just one of the ways those awful spoofs *Date Movie*, *Epic Movie* etc. fail. Just like the classics of the genre (*Airplane!*, *Austin Powers*), *Balls of Fury* has a complete plot with likeable heroes and memorable villains and just happens to have an absurd premise.

At the same time the movie doesn't take itself so seriously that all humor is lost. The blind Master Wong varies between being amazingly perceptive and hopelessly clumsy, FBI Agent Ernie's secret mission with Randy is expected to fail and only a backup plan to more traditional methods. I particularly liked this last point – haven't you ever wondered why engaging Bruce Lee to fight in a to-the-death tournament was considered a better option than just storming and searching the island?

So all the necessary clichés are played out but each one has a humorous twist without being so ridiculous that it makes the movie into "only" a spoof.

Please watch *Balls of Fury*, you most likely won't entirely regret it – you may even love it as I do.

– B. C. Roberts, 2011

-:--:--:--:--:- *GS* -:--:--:--:--:-

Crank (2006) and *Crank 2: High Voltage* (2009)

Written by: Mark Neveldine and Brian Taylor
Directed by: Mark Neveldine and Brian Taylor
Starring: Jason Statham, Amy Smart, Dwight Yoakam

Movie Marathon Category: British Invasion

In Short: Genuinely insane action movies.
Recommended: You may need a penis to enjoy them.

DOC MILES: If you stop, you die.

It is hard to think of a man who epitomizes this month's topic of British Invasion better than Jason Statham. Appearing in thirty-five movies since his debut in *Lock, Stock and Two Smoking Barrels* in 1998, Jason Statham is everywhere and in everything.

Far and away the highlights of this up-and-down ride through action man stardom are the two *Crank* movies. The *Transporter* movies are cool, but nothing tops *Crank* for sheer insanity.

The premise of the first movie is that our lead character, Chev Chelios (Statham), wakes up to find a DVD next to his bed. Slotting it in the drive he learns that some random guy who doesn't like him has snuck into his house and poisoned him while he slept. Naturally, it's not just any poison: this is some "seriously sick Chinese shit." Weirdly, the poison does not kill him instantly, or even quickly, but is instead counteracted by adrenaline. And there's the movie for you. As long as Chev keeps running, jumping, kicking, punching and even sexing, he stays alive.

And what does a hard man like Chev do in such a situation? Well he uses all that running etc. to find the guy who poisoned him and kill him.

This premise takes all of ten minutes to setup and from then on it's a continuous flurry of activity as things get increasingly out of control, culminating in Chev jumping out of a plane and engaging in a mid-air shoot out. Only problem is Chev doesn't have a parachute and the first movie ends SPOILER ALERT with him landing very heavily on the ground after a fall of some many thousands of feet.

But is that enough to keep a crazy man down? Of course not.

And so the second movie opens for us to find Chev being scooped off the road by some medical-looking types who remove his heart to give to some old Chinese boss who clearly needs a new heart from the most badass guy in the city – compatibility notwithstanding, Chev's heart is clearly going to make the old guy stronger, faster, more alive. I would like to say that Chev wakes up before this happens but alas he does not. He only wakes up as they are about to take his impressive appendage – of course, his penis is considerably more important than his heart.

The driving plot device this time is that Chev is wired up with an artificial heart plugged into a car battery. As long as he's powered up, Chev is okay but as soon as the battery starts to drop so does he. Instead of needing to keep his adrenaline pumping, now Chev needs to find increasingly implausible ways to recharge himself – succeeding most spectacularly when he finds a power sub-station.

Again Chev sets out to find the people who did him wrong while he slept (there's an odd Sleeping Beauty analogy thing going here) by hunting his way up the chain of nameless henchmen.

Two supporting roles stand out in these movies. One is Doctor Miles (Dwight Yoakam), who spends each of the movies getting high and laid while providing Chev with begrudging advice on his condition. The world weariness with which he puts down his drink and asks a hooker to get off his lap so he can save Chev's life provides a perfect counter-point to the overcharged rest of the movie.

The second is Chev's ditsy girlfriend Eve (Amy Smart) who is rarely given an explanation for what is going on but agrees to follow Chev around as things get crazier and crazier and twice lets him bang her in public to keep his energy up. Chev's disgust that she is working as a stripper at the start of the second movie (he had apparently disappeared for long enough for her to need some cash) is at odds with his willingness to sexually parade her in public. Eve is great, though, and somehow manages to seem innocent despite all the awfulness around her, not least this insane man who will kill hundreds to find the one person who poisoned him/stole his heart.

These movies are genuinely as ridiculous as action movies in the West get and are approaching the sheer level of zaniness only possible in Eastern Europe and Thailand (*Crank* is about as crazy as *Ong Bak* for you connoisseurs out there). But unlike so many happily B-Grade action movies, the *Crank*s don't get hung up on emotional exposition or any characterization beyond the superficial – none of those things are important when a man is literally alight, burning like a witch on a pyre, and yet still standing and shooting.

So forget that Statham used to be a model for French Connection and forget that his abdominals make all lesser men (which, incidentally, is all of us) feel a little inadequate. Instead, just enjoy the sort of schizophrenic thrills clearly designed for a generation with an attention span of less than two minutes.

(Which, incidentally, is all of us).

– B. C. Roberts, 2011

-:--:--:--:--:- *GS* -:--:--:--:--:-

DOA: Dead or Alive (2006)

Story by: J.F. Lawton
Written by: J.F. Lawton, Adam Gross and Seth Gross
Directed by: Corey Yuen
Starring: Jaime Pressly, Holly Valance, Devon Aoki, Natassia Malthe, Sarah Carter, Eric Roberts

Movie Marathon Category: Video Games

In Short: Far and away the best B-grade movie this side of *The Expendables*. (Which, by the way, also stars Eric Roberts as the bad guy.)

Recommended: Hell, Yes!

> **RYU:** Princess Kasumi, your brother is dead. Your destiny is to lead your people.
> **KASUMI:** I will not believe he is dead, until I see his body.
> **RYU:** There is no body.
> **KASUMI:** Then he is not dead.

- OR -

> **DONOVAN:** Our nanobots were working overtime on that fight.

Forget *Tomb Raider*, forget the *Resident Evil*s, and please god try and forget *Street Fighter: The Legend of Chun-Li*. It is no exaggeration for me to say that *DOA* is clearly the best video game-based movie of all time.

That probably needs a disclaimer. *Dead or Alive 3* and *4* are my two favorite games ever and I have spent more hours on them than should be possible and still have a full-time job... and a wife... let alone a kid. But loving a video game is not a guarantee for loving the movie, for evidence of which, see *Prince of Persia*. (Or, no, don't.)

DOA is a fighting tournament, *Enter the Dragon*-style, to which you can enter only by being generally awesome in a random fight at some opportune point leading up to the tournament. And it probably helps if you manage to win the fight while scantily clad in underwear, a bikini, or super-hot ninja gear.

At the end of said fight, someone with the most amazing aim in the history of the world throws a spinning disk invite which might reach you while sky-diving, or hit the front of your speeding motorcycle, or land on the deck of your boat which is in the middle of the ocean and is the only craft for miles and miles (apart from that of the pirates who unsuccessfully tried to take the boat and were on the other end of a girl in a bikini being awesome in a fight).

14

Of course there is a villain, a man called Donovan (Eric Roberts) who is using the tournament for nefarious purposes. He injects... wait for it... nanobots (of course) into all of the fighters so he can download their moves into his magic sunglasses (I'm not kidding). These sunglasses will make him the greatest fighter in the world and are apparently greatly coveted by wealthy bad people everywhere prepared to pay handsomely for them. Weirdly, they seem to be willing to spend more on the glasses than on guns, which would clearly be more effective, no matter how good of a fighter they made you. Naturally, the beautiful girls all get together to defeat the bad guy, and also save the hot ninja's brother, who got captured by the villain at the last tournament.

The thing about *DOA* is that the plot is extremely straightforward – there are beautiful women who are the good guys and a smarmy old guy who's the bad guy. The women win, all the while being sexy and learning the value of teamwork. At no point in the movie does somebody wake up to find it all a dream, or turn back time, or use any of those convenient plot devices which turn perfectly respectable B-Grade movies into D-Grade disasters. Whenever you're watching an average movie, you're sitting there waiting for it to all get stupid, and it seems that cheap movies are more prone to employ the dodgy plot device for some reason (excluding M. Night Shyamalan movies of course *[Hey! – Ed.]*). I honestly don't know what it is.

But the worst possible sin of a movie based on a video game that is all about fighting is a lack of fighting. Nobody wants a convoluted plot with no action. And this is ultimately where *DOA* delivers most. The movie is a constant stream of increasingly unlikely fights and stunts, from skydiving out of ninja castles to sexy fights in the rain to a random beach volleyball scene straight out of *DOA: Beach Volleyball* to the climax of an exploding temple.

In short, this is 87 minutes of fabulous action that never gets too clever or too stupid.

– B. C. Roberts, 2010

-:--:--:--:--:- *GS* -:--:--:--:--:-

The Fifth Element (1997)

Story by: Luc Besson
Written by: Luc Besson and Robert Mark Kamen
Directed by: Luc Besson
Starring: Bruce Willis, Milla Jovovich, Gary Oldman, Ian Holm, Chris Tucker

Movie Marathon Category: Impending Apocalypse

In Short: A now well-regarded sci-fi avoid-the-apocalypse movie that was once criminally under-rated.
Recommended: Of course.

> **CORNELIUS:** I'm really sorry to have to resort to these methods, Mr. Willis…
> **KORBEN:** Dallas.
> **CORNELIUS:** Er, Mr. Dallas. But we heard about your good luck on the radio, and we need your tickets for Fhloston.
> **KORBEN:** Is this how priests normally take vacations?
> **CORNELIUS:** We're not on a vacation, we're on a mission!
> **KORBEN:** What mission is that?
> **CORNELIUS:** We have to save the world, my son.

I have written about *The Fifth Element* for this magazine before. Just recently I argued in a Geek vs. Geek that this is one of the many sci-fi movies with hopelessly implausible love stories at their center. That being said, there's an awful lot more to *The Fifth Element* than Leeloo (Milla Jovovich) deciding to save the world because Korben Dallas (Bruce Willis) loves her.

The first important thing to know about *The Fifth Element* is that it is a slow movie to get going. For the first hour there is an awful lot of setup as the many different players get into position. On the side of the Great Evil come to wipe out the universe is inter-galactic arms dealer Zorg (Gary Oldman) and the Mangalores (a warrior race that look like a cross between Yoda and a pit bull). On the side of generally saving the universe are Leeloo (whom it later transpires is the titular fifth element); Father Vito Cornelius (Ian Holm), the latest in a long line of priests dedicated to helping the fifth element defeat the Great Evil; and Korben Dallas, former special forces soldier. In between are the government and the military, who generally get in the way.

The second important thing to know is that once the movie gets going, the final forty-five minutes are wall-to-wall action. To defeat the Great Evil, the fifth element needs four stones representing the others (can't have a fifth without a first, second, third and fourth). These stones are lost at the start of the movie but turn out to be held by Diva Plavalaguna, an eight foot tall bright blue opera singer. Strangely, despite carrying the most important objects in the universe, the diva is giving a concert on the holiday satellite Fhloston Paradise which is completely sold out (both the concert and the resort itself). Much of the early action in the movie involves the characters trying to get tickets in order to get there. Ultimately, the government fixes a radio competition so that Dallas wins tickets and can go to the planet to retrieve the stones and save the universe.

Winning the radio competition provides the setup for undoubtedly the movie's highest point: the inclusion of Dallas on the radio show of the androgynous Ruby Rhod (Chris Tucker). Dressed for much of the movie in a fitted red velour cross between a ball gown and a pant-suit, Tucker is a long way from his macho crime fighting James Carter in the *Rush Hour* movies. Ruby broadcasts live as the Diva is killed, Dallas retrieves the stones, and then as Dallas battles and annihilates the Mangalores. Throughout, the President of the Universe and his various underlings listen to the broadcast (it appears to be the central government's only intelligence on Fhloston – surely space-travel level technology gets you some better form of surveillance?) and are suitably horrified by the way Dallas deals with the Mangalores. The highlight of course being:

> **KORBEN:** We need to find the leader. Mangalores
> don't fight without their leaders.
> **AKNOT:** One more shot and we start killing hostages!
> **KORBEN:** That would be the leader.

AKNOT: Send someone in to negotiate!
SHIP OFFICER: I... I never negotiated before.
KORBEN: You mind if... I...?
SHIP OFFICER: Uh... yeah... sure. We're sending someone in to negotiate!
[Korben goes in fires a single shot into Aknot's forehead.]
KORBEN: Anyone else want to negotiate?

Having overcome the bad guys, the crew of good guys set off to activate the fifth element and render the Great Evil harmless. Here the enemy is humanity itself blah blah blah inspirational stuff about love triumphing over hate etc. Long story short, Leeloo and Dallas make out and she decides the universe is worth saving.

Throughout, it is clear that Besson and all the actors aren't taking the movie too seriously, and it is this general underlying sense of frivolity that makes *The Fifth Element* so much fun to watch. Every cliché, like Dallas being the last man in his team left alive, like him leading an unsuccessful civilian life, like the unlikely but necessary chemistry between a beautiful woman and the rugged man who saves her and the universe, is presented knowingly. In this respect it is the exact opposite of the amalgam of military clichés that is *Battle: Los Angeles*.

But in the end, more than anything, the most memorable part of *The Fifth Element* is just how damn stylish it is. Despite being fourteen years old this movie looks good. Really good. Not because the special effects do anything masterful but because, and this is the first and last time you'll ever see me mention this in a film review, the costumes and makeup are pretty much perfect. One of the fashion greats, Jean-Paul Gautier, did the costume design for *The Fifth Element* and it shows. More than any other element of the film, the costumes set up the dystopic futuristic universe – none better than Dallas' orange mesh vest and Leeloo's conveniently placed white bands.

Anyway, before this develops into some way too serious review about costumes, meta-themes and non-diegetic soundtracks it is best to wrap up with one last quote from the movie:

LEELOO: Leeloo Dallas mul-ti-pass. Mul-ti-pass…
KORBEN: Yeah, multipass, she knows it's a
multipass. Leeloo Dallas.

– *B. C. Roberts, 2011*

-:--:--:--:--:- *GS* -:--:--:--:--:-

The Grudge (2004)

Based on *Ju-On* (2000, 2001, 2003), written and directed by
Takashi Shimizu
Written by: Stephen Susco
Directed by: Takashi Shimizu
Starring: Sarah Michelle Gellar, Jason Behr, William Mapother,
KaDee Strickland, Clea DuVall, Bill Pullman.

Movie Marathon Category: Remakes

In Short: Totally respectable but lacking compared to the original.
Recommended: Kind of.

    KAREN: There is something evil there.

A few months ago I reviewed the original Japanese film *Ju-On* for
this magazine and, given this month's topic is remakes, I decided
there was never going to be a better time to see how far short of the
original the American remake falls.

    A friend recently gave me Season 3 of *Buffy: The Vampire Slayer*
(my personal favorite season and the one after which it all goes
wrong) and it reminded me what hot property Sarah Michelle Gellar
once was. This movie was supposed to be her ticket to Hollywood
super-stardom, and cleanse her of the many terrible movie roles she
had had while still starring as Buffy (*Cruel Intentions, Scooby-Doo*).
Though this movie is much better than the latter (hardly surprising),
it's just no real showcase for SMG. It isn't, for example, what *Lost in
Translation* was for Scarlett Johansson.

    In this movie SMG plays Karen, an American in Japan working
for a care center inexplicably staffed by Americans. She is given the

assignment of caring for a catatonic old lady after the previous carer, Yoko (Yoko Maki), fails to show up for a week. We know that Yoko, being peppy and curious, investigated noises in the ceiling and got herself killed by a spooky spirit.

(As an aside, what is it about eternally curious peppy young girls? Where would horror movies be without them?)

The remake stays true to the original and maintains all the scares, which is a good thing. It keeps the disjointed narrative, as well, which culminates in SMG looping back to Bill Pullman (who opened the movie by jumping to his death) discovering the first dead body. Clearly the result of retaining the original director, all these keep the movie from being one of those soulless stupid Hollywood horror remakes like *Dukes of Hazzard* – only kidding, of course I mean *Pulse* (look it up).

The Grudge really should be a movie about Americans abroad. Well it is, but it pretends not to be. The best of this genre, Henry James' *The American*, Oscar Wilde's "The Canterville Ghost" or films like *Lost in Translation* show how Americans fail to fit in – the action is driven by culture clash, it provides meaning to the setting. In *The Grudge*, though the movie is populated by Americans, there is no reason for them to be in Japan (other than the superficial reasons provided in the narrative) and there is no reason for the characters to be American. This is perhaps inevitable given the movie is an extremely faithful remake of the original. In the original, Japanese characters in Japan made perfect sense; in the remake, Americans acting like slightly vaguer white Japanese people leaves this continuing sense of dissonance.

It's difficult to describe, but what pervades the whole movie is a sense of "What are they doing there?" Particularly SMG's boss, Alex (Ted Raimi, best known for his role as the bumbling second sidekick in *Xena: Warrior Princess*). Everyone at all important to the story just happens to be American (apart from the spirits) and everyone else is Japanese. The house SMG visits to care for the old lady is that of an American family who have just moved to Japan for the son's job. His sister is also coincidentally in Japan and becomes a victim of the grudge. The person who discovers the original victims happens to be a visiting American professor. You get the idea.

And the pinnacle of the movie is undoubtedly the explanation provided of the grudge by a Japanese policeman. Doing his best impersonation of Jackie Chan in any of his English speaking movies, the detective explains that when a person dies in 'extleme' circumstances a grudge can be created. Throughout this speech SMG is channeling Cordelia Chase, always trying to look both serious and interested although it's quite clear she has no idea what is going on.

And nor, in the end, do we.

– B. C. Roberts, 2011

-:--:--:--:--:- *GS* -:--:--:--:--:-

Ju-On (2003)

Written by: Takashi Shimizu
Directed by: Takashi Shimizu
Starring: Megumi Okina, Misaki Itô, Misa Uehara, Mariko (no surname, must be the Japanese Madonna)

Movie Marathon Category: Horror

In Short: Scarier than your mama in the morning.
Recommended: Hell Yes (but not for the faint of heart).

HIROHASHI: Thanks for the effort.

I love me a good horror movie. Fans of the genre know that quality horror movies are few and far between but we persist precisely for movies like this.

As a fan of horror, I don't scare easily. I have laughed my way through everything from *Texas Chain Saw Massacre* (imagine the final chase scene with *Benny Hill* music playing – absolutely hilarious) to *Dawn of the Dead* (there's something about that bad 70s make-up that makes me giggle). But there was no laughing with *Ju-on*.

The movie follows a haunted house. *Ju-on* roughly translates as Curse or Grudge (as the Hollywood remake was called) – with the Curse created by the murder of Kayako Shibata (Mariko), killed by her husband and now exacting post-mortem revenge on the world. Anyone who comes in contact with the house is cursed and they can then pass that curse onto others. So it's really a domino effect of supernatural badness.

But what makes this movie so different to every other fright-fest out there? Ju-on was originally made as two short, straight to video releases on a tiny budget. The consequent minimalism was maintained when Shimizu turned the two shorts into the theatrical release. So *Ju-on* focuses very tightly on characters and a small number of extremely creepy locations. Most of the movie is set in the one haunted house in Nerima, a suburb of Tokyo, and as the movie goes on and it becomes clearer how the curse works, there is a tension associated with anyone entering the house. As different characters are drawn towards the house we will them not to knock on the door, to ignore the voice of the ghostly little boy, to walk away and stay safe. My reaction to this house reminds me of the first time I watched *Psycho* as a young teenager – practically pleading with Sam and Lila not to go into the basement. You know that the danger is entirely avoidable though, of course, few of the characters ever manage to avoid it.

When I first watched this movie it was on those old VCDs you used to buy in Asia before DVDs had conquered the world. So my new wife and I were sitting in a dark room and when we came to the end of the first VCD the whole room went black. Neither of us would move. Sure, we wanted to know what happened but how could we be sure that there wasn't a dangerously quiet ten-year waiting in the darkness to pass on the curse and send his vengeful mother after us? The truth was that we couldn't but I manned-up, changed the disc and was all the more surprised when things got much scarier.

One of the really disturbing elements of *Ju-on* is the way that certain horror movie tropes are ignored. Almost all great horror stories take place at night – if not the entire movie then certainly the pivotal moments. Daylight is a time of relative safety in the horror world. Not so here. Kayako strikes people in the middle of the day – once cursed there is no place of safety. But the *coup de grace* occurs when Kayako has pursued her target (Nishina Rika, played by Megumi Okina) through the streets and then along the corridors of Rika's apartment block all the while making an unsettling croaking noise. Rika runs into her apartment and pulls the bed covers over her head. In a scene surely calculated to terrify everyone in the audience who will be cowering in their beds after watching the movie, Kayako crawls out from under the bedcovers and kills Rika. My wife maintains that this scene is just pure sadism on the part of the director against his audience.

Like all great movies it is hard to explain the appeal of *Ju-on*. It is clever, suspenseful and terrifying in equal measure and avoids the melodramatic theatricality which makes so many horror movies laughable.

If you only watch one Japanese horror movie this Halloween, make it *Ju-on*.

– B. C. Roberts, 2010

-:--:--:--:--:- *GS* -:--:--:--:--:-

Spider-Man (2002)

Created by Stan Lee and Steve Ditko
Screenplay by: David Koepp
Directed by: Sam Raimi
Starring: Tobey Maguire, Willem Dafoe, Kirsten Dunst, Cliff Robertson, James Franco

Movie Marathon Category: Comic Books

In Short: You can leave your mask on.
Recommended: Yes.

> **PETER PARKER:** Whatever life holds in store for me, I will never forget these words: "With great power comes great responsibility." This is my gift, my curse. Who am I? I'm Spider-Man.

I have been waiting for an opportunity to review the *Spider-Man* movies. In truth, I'm always looking for any forum at all to discuss Spider-Man. In the mid-80s I was a little boy running around in a Spider-Man costume. Through the 90s I was a teenager wishing I could get bitten by a radioactive or genetically modified spider – I didn't mind which as long as the result was all the powers of a spider in a handily anthropomorphized form (that is, no extra legs or eyes – just stronger and better). In the late 90s, when I was young and inspired I got a Spider-Man tattoo.

When I was walking out of the midnight session of the first *Spider-Man* movie in 2002, I overheard the following conversation between two sixteen year old girls:

> **GIRL 1:** That was the most awesome movie, like, ever.
> **GIRL 2:** I know! Like whatever. We should totally go get Spider-Man tattoos.
> **GIRL 1:** OMG! Totally.

It didn't quite prompt me to go get mine lasered off, but I do hope those girls never made it to the tattoo parlor.

Now, I really love origin movies (apart from *X-Men Origins: Wolverine*). I love the way we get to see an ordinary person become a superhero and the way they struggle with the transition. And the constant in all origin movies is that the hero has to give something up to be super – normally the girl. It seems that unless you're Tony Stark, superhero-dom is a major barrier to a fulfilling love life.

Which makes no sense whatsoever.

Spider-Man begins with the line: "This story, like all worth telling, is about a girl." But this is clearly a lie. Mary Jane Watson (Kirsten Dunst), beautiful though she is, exists as a character only so that Peter Parker (Tobey Maguire) can idolize her and then fail to capitalize on his awesome superpowers. Superman always understood that the correct way to woo an interested female was to take them flying – that's pretty hard for others to compete with. But Peter Parker really lacks a certain *joie de vivre*.

I understand that Peter's beloved Uncle Ben (Cliff Robertson) is killed as a (tenuous) consequence of his acting like the kick-ass

24

superhero he could be, but there is surely a middle way between being completely reckless with his loved ones and relinquishing the prospect of sexy times with Mary Jane just to protect her from some nebulous threat.

This noble behavior is misplaced because, as we all know, the superhero's loved ones are never safe, whether s/he reveals her/his alter-ego or not. Keeping Spidey a secret does not protect Mary Jane in the second movie, so why not be out with it now? Or just give up on the childhood crush and find a girl who lets him keep the mask on? (I'm sure there would be plenty of takers.)

Which brings us to the major problem that many superhero movies encounter: having either the hero or the alter-ego be much more interesting than the other. I always found Tony Stark much more interesting than Iron Man, but Bruce Wayne is so much less engaging than Batman. In the Spider-Man universe, Spidey is really the better character. Peter Parker is anxiety-ridden, timid, always trying so hard to do the right thing, but Spider-Man … Spider-Man gets to swing across Manhattan Island on a couple of web-slingers and pash *[translation for our non-Australian friends: make out with. – Ed.]* the random girls he saves. It's no coincidence that Mary Jane falls in love with Spidey first – when Peter puts on the mask he stops whining and starts fixing. Just like his adversary in this movie, the Green Goblin (Willem Dafoe), Peter Parker is better and stronger as his masked self. Which says something profound about how putting a mask on gives us an opportunity to escape our weaknesses.

But what this movie could be about is how one guy went from being hopeless, from failing to fulfill any of the socially designated indicators of excellence, to being awesome. Not through any skill on his part, but instead as the result of an opportune spider bite.

And that's the take-home message of this movie: the next time you're on a school trip in a strange lab, make sure you're the one who gets bitten by the creepy looking arachnid. It could change your life. Or it could keep your life exactly the same, except with more angsting. Your choice.

– B. C. Roberts, 2010

-:--:--:--:--:- *GS* -:--:--:--:--:-

Underworld (2003)

Story by: Kevin Grevioux, Len Wiseman and Danny McBride
Teleplay by: Danny McBride
Directed by: Len Wiseman
Starring: Kate Beckinsale, Scott Speedman, Michael Sheen, Shane Brolly, Bill Nighy

Movie Marathon Category: Beginnings

In Short: Kate Beckinsale in leather. You need more?
Recommended: Yes.

> **SELENE:** Whether you like it or not, you're in the middle of a war that has been raging for the better part of a thousand years. A blood feud between vampires and lycans. Werewolves.

Underworld, like so many excellent genre movies, starts out with a simplicity which threatens to run into the mundane. Vampires and werewolves have been at war for centuries and that conflict continues today. Cue a series of increasingly bloody battles between the two in exciting modern locales and you have *Blade* with werewolves and a leather-clad, super-hot Kate Beckinsale. Honestly, they probably would have been onto a winner with just that.

But unlike the worst entries in the genre (I'm looking at you, *Van Helsing*), *Underworld* turns a simple premise into a solid foundation and comes up with a tale which is more interesting for its political intrigue than it is for the predominantly well-choreographed fight scenes. There's a secret deal between the vampire aptly named Kraven (Shane Brolly) and the leader of the Lycans, Lucian (Michael Sheen); the awakening of a fabulously mean vampire elder Viktor played by Bill Nighy (who is fast replacing Christopher Walken as the king of the minor, though pivotal, role); and the womanly machinations of the terrifically ambitious Erika (Sophia Myles).

I first watched *Underworld* when my son was three weeks old. Appallingly sleep deprived, awake at 4am, this movie is forever tinged with delirium for me. Having re-watched it more than once since, an element of confusion remains, which in many ways adds to why I like it. Kate Beckinsale's Selene is the good soldier, loyal to the elders and the most committed killer of Lycans. Without a single change of facial expression, she falls in love with a human, then continues to protect him when he turns into a Lycan, even to the point of killing other vampires. After a quick word from the now treacherous Kraven she withdraws her loyalty, her patriarch Viktor admits he killed her family (despite managing to keep the secret for six hundred years) and she kills Viktor, the very elder she awoke in order to protect her coven. Still without a single movement of facial muscles.

I like to think that all this merely enhances the mystique of our dour hero; that she can make momentous or foolhardy decisions with the same implacable face despite the emotions coursing underneath. This way Selene stands with the long line of heroes who made the tough choices despite high personal cost (like Buffy sending Angel to Hell, or Sarah Connor giving up her parental rights, or Spidey... well, doing anything ever).

Otherwise we are left with only two choices. Either Kate Beckinsale belongs to the Jennifer Love Hewitt school of acting (find one look, maintain indefinitely), or the plot of *Underworld* does not actually make all that much sense. I am fairly sure the first option is false because Beckinsale manages to show plenty of emotion in *Much Ado About Nothing* when her character, Hero, is dumped by the ludicrously gullible and naïve Claudio. And it would be unfortunate to accept the second option, even though there is a niggling feeling that maybe characters true to their history would have acted quite differently. Why Viktor admits to killing Selene's family continues to baffle me.

Still, watch this movie if you haven't already. Watch it for the clever plot, some fabulous characters and an extremely satisfying final action sequence. But as with so many genre flicks, try not to think too hard about what is happening in front of you because in the end, a little too much credulity is asked of Selene—and, it must be said, the audience.

– B. C. Roberts, 2010

TV

Terminator: The Sarah Connor Chronicles (2008 – 2009)

Based on: *Terminator* (1984) etc.
Created by: Josh Friedman
Starring: Lena Headey, Thomas Dekker, Summer Glau, Brian Austin Green
Number of Episodes: 31 (2 Seasons)
2008 - 2009

In Short: Apart from the new *Doctor Who* absolutely the best sci-fi show on television in the last decade.
Recommended: Hell Yes.

> **SARAH:** Every family has rules, and we had ours. Keep your head down. Keep your eyes up. Resist the urge to be seen as important or special. Know your exits.

I like to think of myself as your moderate geek, a center-left geek. The geek who delves a bit further into sci-fi than just watching *Star Wars*, but is not a rabid fan on a bulletin board arguing for Kataang or Zatara.

But *Terminator: The Sarah Connor Chronicles* turns me into that crazy fan. The one who can't have a reasonable discussion in public, who can't be trusted not to yell at the poor person who suggests that Fox was right to axe *Sarah Connor* in favor of *Dollhouse*. *[I remember! – Ed.]*

Until *Sarah Connor*, the *Terminator* universe was more exciting for its potential than for anything that actually appeared on the silver screen. Go back and watch *The Terminator* or *Terminator 2: Judgment Day* now and you will see two quite awful examples of silly sci-fi movies. But the premise, the core idea was always fascinating: humans are at war with machines in the future and that war has spilled out into the past, as agents from each side seek to change their (future) present.

Sarah Connor was too short-lived. We got a season and a half of it – the first cut short by the 2008 Writers' Strike – a paltry 31 episodes. The series is kind of set after *Terminator 3: Rise of the Machines*, though not really. Most of the series takes place in 2008-9, five years after the events in the third movie. But in the first episode of the series Sarah Connor (Lena Headey) and John Connor (Thomas Dekker), along with the hottest Terminator in the history of Terminator-ness, Cameron (Summer Glau), jump from 1999, thereby avoiding the events of *Terminator 3: Rise of the Machines* (in which Judgment Day occurs).

So the series follows the adventures of a 16-year-old John as he, his mother and their pet Terminator attempt to stay alive and track down any element which might one day support the machines. The first season is great, as we see Sarah, John and Cameron adjusting to the future and re-establishing semi-normal lives. But the second season is where things really heat up. And amazingly, the driving force behind this is really the inclusion of *Beverley Hills 90210* alumnus Brian Austin Green as Derek Reese (John's uncle), who looks rugged enough to warrant dating Megan Fox. Derek is a human sent back with a list of companies and people who need to be stopped to weaken Skynet and the machines – this list provides much of the action until Derek's girlfriend from the future, Jesse (Stephanie Chaves-Jacobsen), turns up with her own plan to change the future course of the war.

And so the story becomes about relationships. Derek and Jesse, in love with each other but completely unable to trust each other with the details of their "work"; John and Sarah, struggling with the typical teenager issues heightened by periodic visits from killer robots; John and his girlfriend Riley (Leven Rambin), who form a love triangle along with Cameron the robot. In every relationship someone is hiding at least one thing and every interaction is fraught with what isn't being confessed. By the end, the fight against the machines is just a background for the compelling interpersonal interactions. And when everything went wrong towards the end of the second season I became that rabid fan telling anyone who would listen that John and Cameron were destined to be together and that it

29

was amazingly important, that the fate of the world depended on everything turning out all right for the Connors.

Sarah Connor is the rare series that rouses passion in the usually dispassionate, and that is perhaps the best recommendation I can give.

– B. C. Roberts, 2010

-:--:--:--:--:- *GS* -:--:--:--:--:-

GEEK VS. GEEK

Copyright Protection: Patently Absurd by B. C. Roberts

It is in many ways difficult to debate the merits of intellectual property. Intellectual property is a topic of some vastness incorporating copyright, patents, and trademarks, along with specific legislative schemes for things like circuit designs and common law actions like passing off. We can ignore these latter schemes as being extremely complex and not covering the sorts of creative outputs relevant to this debate. Further, there is little that is controversial about trademarks (except for trademarks on common words like Harry Potter), so we will leave it to one side as well. Patents are so irremediably broken as a way of dealing with inventions – most particularly pharmaceuticals – that it hardly seems like an argument worth making. I direct you to every human rights article written on access to medications in the developing world to deal with that topic. Only someone who supports having children die of preventable causes supports patent protection as it currently exists in the world.

Which leaves us with copyright protection. Though intellectual property commenced life in 1624 in England with the Statute of Monopolies, that statute only covered patents and not copyright. The first copyright statute was the Statute of Ann in 1709, which prohibited the unauthorized copying of books. Before this time, governments in Europe would provide monopoly rights to print a book to a particular printer, but this was part of a regime of censorship whereby individual book printers and booksellers were licensed by the city and that license would be revoked if they were found to publish work critical of the government. The Statute of Ann granted copyright privileges for 14 years for new books and 21 years for books already in print.

Which is all a nice history lesson, but let's get to the point. What are the aims of intellectual property protection and does the current regime effectively achieve those aims? The aims of copyright protection from the first legislation through to today can be summarized under two headings:

1. To compensate the creators of creative works for their investment in the creation
2. To incentivize the creation of creative works

Now, if intellectual property protection does not achieve these aims, we can safely conclude that the existing regime is a failure. I follow the critical theorist Raymond Geuss in rejecting the need to provide an alternative scheme – the claim that one cannot criticize the status quo without an alternative is how those who benefit from the status quo put off criticism.

On to the aims.

1. Does intellectual property compensate creators of creative works for their investment in the creation?

The first thing we need to consider under this heading is the way in which copyright provides financial compensation. When one creates a work one is granted a monopoly right over the reproduction of that creative work. Copyright does not protect the characters created (hence fan fiction) but only the specific expression of the work. This does extend cross-media so that a person cannot make a film which is substantially similar to someone's book, or a song from a painting and so on. This monopoly right is granted for the life of the author of the work PLUS an additional fifty years; conceivably, this can amount to well over one hundred years of protection (a good deal longer than the Statute of Ann – which, incidentally, was the law in force when writers like Wordsworth, Keats, and Jane Austen were writing).

Now, nothing in the provision of this level of protection examines the actual investment of the authors in their creation of the work. A piece of awful self-indulgent Plath-esque poetry written by a depressed teenager in English class is granted exactly the same level of protection as a multi-volume history of the Roman Empire. If the aim were really to compensate for investment and effort, we might expect any consideration at all of the actual effort expended in the awarding of protection.

2. Does the provision of intellectual property protection incentivize the creation of creative works?

The most enduring argument for intellectual property protection is that if authors/inventors are not provided with a monopoly right over their creation, then they will not create, and the world will be a worse place for the lack of arts and inventions. This argument is patently absurd (please pardon the pun).

Every single day people write amazing works of admirable sophistication and post them to the internet for people to read freely. None expect to receive financial compensation for their work; they write to express themselves, to tell stories to be involved with groups of like-minded individuals. More fan fiction is written than original fiction; clearly, there are other incentives at play here.

My favorite example of the stupidity of the incentive argument is that almost all of the people who actually create medical breakthroughs receive no money for them. Almost all medical research work is performed by researchers in universities and drug companies who do not get to own the intellectual property of their own creations (that going to their employers instead). Professors in university search for a cure for cancer not because they will be rich (because they won't) but so they can be the person who cured cancer. And, no offence, but the work to cure cancer is considerably more important than works of popular fiction. If these people will provide medical breakthroughs without intellectual property incentives, surely we can expect Joss Whedon to get over me downloading an episode or two of *Buffy*.

To go back to fan fiction: though you might concede that people write without financial incentive, you might also suggest they would be mortified if their work was copied and passed off as being someone else's. This surely is proof that people care about copyright. Maybe, but not quite. Passing somebody's work off as your own is rightly the target of moral censure and the reason we have the pejorative term "plagiarism." We don't need 100 years of copyright protection to defend against plagiarism – and anyway, what possible harm can plagiarism cause after we are dead? In a school, if a student plagiarizes they usually fail or are required to resubmit. If they were pursued for breach of copyright, the original author would be entitled

33

to damages for lost revenue. Ummm. That seems to be kind of a problem, since in most of these cases the work being plagiarized wasn't going to make any money. Plus, who on earth would want to launch expensive legal proceedings because somebody copied their essay about the unseen vampire in "The Fall of the House of Usher"? And it holds true in fan fiction as well. When somebody copies another person's work, the original author wants "justice" in the form of an apology, a retraction, and recognition of themselves as the true author of the work – preferably as quickly as possible. The legal protection of intellectual property rights simply does not provide that.

So where are we at? The two rationales normally put forward to justify intellectual property just do not fly. It does not compensate people based on effort and people clearly do not need copyright or the promise of riches to inspire creative works.

There are a couple more arguments to deal with before we can finish, though. One is the issue of stealing from artists; the second is the problems associated with intellectual property rights. Let's look at the latter first.

Copyright is a legal right. It is not some free-standing moral principle. What that means is that if you believe your rights have been violated, get prepared to go to court. This is shit for the artist seeking to protect their work because it is a huge waste of time and money and unless you are super successful (at which point I don't properly understand why you care so much: Anne Rice, do you really need another mansion?); legal proceedings are pretty much prohibitively expensive. And it is worse for the individual who has downloaded the work who is now treated like an awful criminal. I think everyone agrees that paying $200,000 in damages for downloading a few songs off Limewire is a total overreaction and completely disproportionate to the damage suffered by the artist.

The other thing about the legality of intellectual property is that the rights granted are, by their very nature, assignable. What that means is that some bunch of douchebags running a record company make all the money while the artists receive somewhere between twenty cents and a dollar for each album sold. This is not some contingent corollary of the existing system – it is necessitated by the status of intellectual property as rights. Just look at every other type of property in the world.

Which brings us nicely to the issue of stealing from artists. The single group of people most responsible for stealing from artists are publishers, be they book publishers, record companies, or whoever. When I found out about the two zombie books written by my adversary in this debate under the pseudonym Mira Grant, the first thing I did was go to a torrent site and download them. Then, of course, our illustrious Editor-in-Chief was outraged and sent me an Amazon voucher and told me to buy them all legit-like. Which, incidentally, I did. But I would love to know how much of the twenty dollars I spent on Amazon actually went to the author. And then I would much prefer to send that money directly to the author (though I'm not sure you can Western Union amounts under a dollar) and not subsidize some fuckwit editor's coke habit.

In summary: for the first time in history, the internet is making it possible for the creators of works to connect directly with their public. And some are starting to do so. When Radiohead released their album *In Rainbows* online with a "pay what you think it's worth" price, they sold considerably fewer copies than they had of earlier albums and yet made considerably more money. Artists and writers who hang onto copyright as their way of doing business are just as anachronistic as the MPAA going after every person who downloads a song illegally. Why stay beholden to publishers who see artists as product to be sold? Especially if you are offering online versions anyway?

Intellectual property is obsolete when it comes to copyright (and patents are downright murderous).

– B. C. Roberts, 2011

-:--:--:--:--:- *GS* -:--:--:--:--:-

Copyright Protection: Theft is Theft is Theft by Seanan McGuire

Okay, wow. First off, a few statements:

1. I am pro-copyright. (There's a shocker.) I am pro-copyright both because I work VERY HARD to create the things I create, and

because I enjoy having this mysterious ability I call "feeding my cats." They are all the size of small yeti. If I don't feed them, they will devour me.

2. Being pro-copyright is not the same thing as being pro-endless extensions of the initial copyright law, la la la, let's keep this bitch in a box forever. While I wouldn't necessarily be thrilled about going back to a twenty-one year copyright period for new books, I'd be perfectly happy with life of the author plus ten years for the estate to get itself in order. Saying that being pro-copyright means you're in favor of every copyright extension forced through by corporate interests is a bit of a misnomer.

3. I do not think the word "incentive" means what my adversary thinks it does.

Let's discuss.

Author Compensation, or, Feeding My Cats

According to my adversary, one of the reasons that copyright doesn't work is because it doesn't pay out in a way which is matched to the effort put forth by the creator.

So, here's the thing. If I spend five years writing a book that is like removing a bone from my living flesh, leaving gaping wounds and lots of blood behind, and you spend three weeks writing a book that flows through you like a wind from Heaven, and the books are of equal quality, we will get paid roughly the same by traditional publishing for our books. My book represented a great deal more in the way of time and effort, but publishing, like the honey badger, doesn't give a shit; publishing wants to see the pages.

In a way, writing is a lot like being on a reality show. I watch *America's Next Top Model* pretty faithfully, and every cycle, there's a girl who doesn't really have to do anything. The judges call them "natural models," and while they don't usually win (they're not dramatic enough to take home that brass ring), they almost always go on to healthy careers in the modeling industry. Other girls struggle and fight for every photo shoot. And if you don't watch the episodes—if you just look at the pictures they post at the end, showing the "best shots" of the week—you can't tell those girls apart.

The amount of effort they put out is extraneous. The finished product is what matters.

My books are pretty straight-up genre fiction. I write urban fantasy and I write science fiction; they're mass-market paperbacks; you can find them on the shelf at your local S-Mart. The first volume of my October Daye series, *Rosemary and Rue*, represented ten years of work. No, you didn't read that wrong. TEN YEARS. Ten years is a very long time. And while I won't say that I would have been sad if my publisher had gone "wow, ten years, here's a million dollars," I'm not upset that they didn't do that, either. The fact that I had to learn how to write a good book does not mean they need to pay for my learning curve.

The most recent October Daye book, *One Salt Sea*, took about eight months to write; most of the reviews agree that it's the best book in the series so far, which I find reassuring, since any creator wants to improve. But eight months is a lot less than ten years! Should I have received eighty cents for every ten dollars that I was paid for the first book? Would that be what's fair here?

I write distressingly fast under any circumstances; sometimes this makes me do more work, since I overshoot my marks, but once I learn where those marks are, I get very good at hitting them every time, and I do so very, very quickly. Some of my best friends are the same way. Some of my other friends move more slowly, at everything from a stroll to a creep. They invest more time in their work. They invest more hours of their lives. Do they deserve to be better compensated, since I just "dashed it off," while they really worked?

The question of effort-for-compensation is something which arises only in the creative fields. People don't refuse to pay for their furniture because it was put together by a team of factory workers, none of whom put forth a huge amount of specific effort; they don't refuse to buy toys because they were made by machines. Higher quality things will wind up being worth more, and there is no direct correlation between "took longer to make/took more effort" and "better end result."

People Give Away Fanfic for Free, and That Means Copyright Is Useless

My path to becoming a professional author followed the path tread by so many before me: I wrote fan fiction. I wrote lots and lots and buckets and buckets of fan fiction, and I posted (or published—I overlapped the era of the paper 'zine, even if only by a few years) my work for free. I was drunk on creation, and those were wonderful days. You can probably find my fanfic if you look, and you can still read it totally for free. Just please remember that you're looking at a span of creative development that lasted about fifteen years, okay? Some of it is ass.

When I was working in other people's worlds I, like everyone else in my community, knew that I didn't own these characters. I didn't own these settings. What I owned was my own unique approach to them, and that was the "product" I had to "sell." I sold it! I had a wonderful time selling it. And never once did I think "oh, wow, the quality of this piece of *Buffy the Vampire Slayer* fic is so great that the original work is no longer owned by Joss Whedon."

Fanfic is successful for the same reason that works like *Shakespeare in Love* or *Pride and Prejudice and Zombies* are successful: because it gives us something familiar to hold onto the second we walk through the door. When I sit down to write a piece of fanfic, I don't have to capture or entice my audience. I already have them. I say "this is a piece of *Barry Ween* fic," and lead off with "Boy, eighteen, hair in spikes, eyes like holes," and they already know that I'm writing a story set after the original series. They know that Barry is still going crazy. They know so much, because it was handed to them by our shared cultural base in the original series.

Very few of the people I know go out and read fic based on series they don't already follow, unless they are following the author of that fic. In that way, fanfic writers become a weird sort of ad exec, selling other people's dreams by showing them through the prisms of their own.

I am not going to claim that fic requires no work: I wrote it, I know it requires work. I am not going to claim that it's the easy way out: I dare anyone to read some of the truly transformative, introspective material that's out there and say that anything about it is "easy." But I am going to say that, because we have a pre-existing relationship with the settings, we are more willing to walk through that door, and that saves the fanfic author a certain level of work in trying to lure us in.

A better example of people giving something creative away online for free, while also getting buy-in for a universe that requires that lure, would be the web comic. Web comics are very rarely derivative (anymore—many early web comics were basically fanfic with pictures), and are often based around very complicated, original worlds. While there have been, and continue to be, pay sites, web comics continue to proliferate, and even to thrive. Isn't that a ringing condemnation of copyright?

Nope. Most really successful web comics have healthy merchandise lines of T-shirts, books, mouse pads, even jewelry and plush toys. They make back their time investment on sales and in-page advertising. Even the "big kids" of the web comic world have figured out how to monetize their landscape, and have, in so doing, really recreated the TV advertising and merchandising model. They're not books. They're shows that move very, very slowly.

Thirty Minutes or It's Free

One huge freedom of fanfic that I no longer have was partial posting. When I was working on a really long story, I could put it up one chapter at a time, essentially serializing it. I was able to share my work slowly, and people were always grateful for the next piece. Try doing that with something that's been paid for. No, really. I dare you. Unless you're working in an inherently serial medium, like television or web comics (both graphic, rather than purely textual), you're going to have issues.

"Crowd-funded novels" often follow the one chapter at a time model, not releasing the next piece until it's been paid for. This is about the only way you're going to see the piecemeal approach working in original fiction. Which takes us back to the "fanfic is free, why isn't your novel?" My novel isn't free because I had to write all fifty chapters before I was allowed to publish it, and that took time and effort and editing and sleepless nights and anxiety and a lot of other things.

When I take the money, I take the deadlines. When I take the deadlines, I take the copyright protection, too. I am a protected investment, and I am okay with that.

Pathogen Party!

You may not know this, but I study infectious diseases for fun. So when I was reading my adversary's initial argument, and hit this piece, I choked on my soda. To wit:

> *"My favorite example of the stupidity of the incentive argument is that almost all of the people who actually create medical breakthroughs receive no money for them."*

I...uh...WHAT?!

Those people are being paid for their work. They are doing the scientific equivalent of "work for hire," like when a good friend of mine gets paid to write *Star Wars* novels, the copyrights on which she does not own. I want to write media tie-in novels for a show called *Haven* someday, just because I love it, and if I do that, I will not own those copyrights.

Disney animators don't own the characters they're paid to help design. Chris Saunders is one of my personal heroes, and he doesn't own Stitch, the little blue alien that he created. Why? Because they were on salary to create. If you want to pay me eighty thousand dollars a year to create something for you, I'll create it, and the fact that I won't own that copyright is not proof that the system doesn't work.

Arts and sciences are connected, but they have never been identical. Saying that someone will work toward a cure for cancer without compensation is not the same thing as saying that I should finish my series without a guarantee of compensation. As my adversary says, curing cancer is more important. If I cure cancer, I have a lifetime of paid speaking engagements and Nobel Prizes ahead of me. If I finish this book, I have the hope that I will get to write another book. That's it.

Oh, and Theft is Theft is Theft

Again to quote:

> *"To go back to fan fiction: though you might concede
> that people write without financial incentive you might
> also suggest they would be mortified if their work was
> copied and passed off as being someone else'."*

You want to see vicious? Watch a fanfic community where someone has just used someone else's OC (original character) without permission. Fanfic is not plagiarism. Plagiarism is not fanfic. Attempting to conflate the two at this stage just muddies the waters—and every fanfic author I've ever met who was plagiarized has brought the hammer of censure down hard. Maybe they didn't get monetary compensation the way that they would have if they'd been working for pay, but their grievances were heard.

Why the Successful Sue?

My adversary very accurately states that if you believe your rights have been violated, you'd better get prepared to go to court. He then asks why the really successful people—the ones who can win—bother, since what, do they need another mansion? The answer is simple: they bother because they can win. They bother because I, as a relatively new author, can't win. They are acting to protect the industry as a whole, and yeah, they're probably a little upset, since nobody likes to be stolen from.

(I am aware that not every illegal download is the equivalent of a sale. I am also, sadly, aware that my speaking out on the pro-copyright side means that a great many people will probably go "yay, let's torrent her work, that'll show her." To those people I say: please don't. Please stop, and consider that I have cats to feed, I have a mortgage to pay, and I don't come into your home or office and steal the value of your work. Just because I would never have let you clean my teeth, style my hair, or fix my car if I couldn't make you do it for free, that won't make it less of a theft.)

People who stand a chance in hell of winning these suits bring them because they want to make it clear that things have consequences. Maybe you violate my copyrights a thousand times and not get caught. Maybe you'll get caught the thousand and first time…and maybe that will be the time when I'm in a position to sue. Do you really want to roll those dice?

Stealing from Artists

My adversary says, again, quoting: "The single group of people most responsible for stealing from artists are publishers, be they book publishers, record companies or whoever."

He follows this up with, "When I found out about the two zombie books written by my adversary, the first thing I did was go to a torrent site and download them."

Um. Gee, thanks?

My publishers do not steal from me. My publishers pay me to do the thing I love. My publishers are also a business, and they have associated operating costs. Let's look at what it costs to make a book appear on a torrent site, shall we?

Advance to author.
Editorial review.
Copyediting.
Commission of artwork.
Cover design.
Printing.
Shipping and storage.
Advertising.

All these things make the book not suck. What other costs does my publisher have?

Rent.
Salaries.
Health insurance.
Internet and phones.
Electricity.

I am happy to have my publisher use me to make money to keep the lights on so that they can keep printing the books I love to write. It's an ecological balance, and no, I am not stolen from or screwed.

And none of my editors have coke habits, despite my adversary's implication.

How much did I make when he finally bought those books of mine legitimately? About seventy-five cents a copy. Not a huge amount, I admit. But I got an advance from my publisher, and I sell a lot of books because I have a publisher. My first book—the one where I had no name recognition at all—sold more copies in its first week than my most popular fanfic ever had hits. The scale is very different.

Would Radiohead have made all that money for *In Rainbows* if they hadn't started out in traditional music publishing? No. I don't think so.

Copyright can be abused. Copyright should not be used to punish fanfic authors or to beat people like a club. But it should be used to protect creators, and it should keep my work mine until my death, if not after. The arguments used to justify violation of copyright have a lot in common with the arguments I used to get from the kids I went to school with when they wanted my lunch—"I want it, you have it, it should be mine, it's not fair." I worked for that lunch. I worked for my copyrights.

Please stop arguing that I shouldn't be allowed to feed my cats just because you've decided this is a brave new world.

– Seanan McGuire, 2011

-:--:--:--:--:- *GS* -:--:--:--:--:-

Harry Potter: Over-Rated and Just Not Very Good by K. Burtt

There hasn't been a book series in recent memory that has made as profound an impact on the world as J. K. Rowling's *Harry Potter*.

This depresses me.

There are a great many books and book series which are better-written and more enjoyable for both kids and adults that now seem to be shuffled to the side, discounted, and/or otherwise had their significance reduced or ignored due to the sheer amount of press that *Harry Potter* has received.

Now, I will say upfront that I don't completely hate the *Harry Potter* series. The first few books were decent for what they were, and it's not like I would rather have my armpits infested with the fleas of a thousand camels than even think about reading a *Harry Potter* book again, but the series overall is so fraught with issues and problems (and I say that not just because it is fun to use the word "fraught") that I find it quite undeserving of the praise and hype that still gets heaped upon it.

So here, presented to you in some kind of particular order (though what kind of order is up to you to determine), are all the various reasons why I find the *Harry Potter* book series to be completely overrated and just not very good.

The Main Character

Yes, Harry himself — he who managed to get his name at the beginning of the title of every single adventure (not even Indiana Jones managed that feat!). I don't think he makes a good main character, for a few different reasons. For one, he's not really that good at anything. Okay, yes, he is good at flying, I grant you that, and one could claim that he is also good at the Patronus charm, though I could counter that by saying that was just a function of him being taught it earlier than the rest of his class and having the chance to practice. Other than that, what was he good at? Magic? Schoolwork? Mischief? It always seemed that all other characters just assume that he's good at any/all of the above, so there never is any reason for him to actually *be* good at any/all of the above. I'm not saying that he necessarily should be, or that the main character in general needs to be "The Best" or anything, but throughout the series, Harry is touted by others as being a wonderful and excellent wizard for no discernible reason.

What also bugs me is how it seems most everything that occurs for Harry is directly due to others. Hermione is the power behind most magic and essentially all schoolwork; Harry's skill at sneaking around is solely due to his invisibility cloak (with help from the Marauder's Map – now that's a nifty piece of work; why couldn't

Harry and his friends try to create something like that?!); and even his defeats of Voldemort are due to outside circumstances.

But all this, annoying as it is, wouldn't necessarily be a huge problem if it weren't for Harry's attitude.

His attitude, particularly in the middle books, removed any sense of connection I felt with the character. For a series to work, one needs to like the protagonist, and starting in the fourth book, there is little to like. I found his apathy in *Goblet of Fire* to be rather grating — here he is in what is supposed to be this grand spectacle and trial of wizarding (more on that later. Oooh... foreshadowing), and he does... nothing. He has to be hand-held and guided through the entire thing. Granted, he is participating in the Tri-Wizard Tournament (Quad-Wizard Tournament?) against his will, but couldn't he at least try to put in a little more effort himself to be prepared for the various tasks considering how "dangerous" they were?

But apathetic Book 4 Harry doesn't hold a candle to angry, arrogant, bratty Book 5 Harry. If apathetic Harry made me similarly apathetic toward him, angry Harry made me actively dislike him. After all he has gone through in the previous books to that point, don't you think that he would take a second to attempt to look at the bigger picture and not be so completely selfish? Perhaps try trusting Dumbledore? Stop lashing out at his friends?

"But wait!" you say, "He's just acting out like a normal teenager would!"

Ah, I'm glad that you brought that up, as that brings me to my next problem with the series.

The Transition from Children's to Young Adult to Adult

Since when is Harry a normal teenager? Considering the circumstances, his sullen, bitter, sulking self just seems out of character. But it's just a symptom of a bigger issue. As the series progresses, J.K. Rowling tries to transition from a Children's series to a Young Adult series to a more Adult series, and she isn't particularly successful at doing so. Children's literature is full of black and white situations. The good guys are obviously good, the bad guys are evil caricatures, and the situations are regularly completely and unreasonably over-the-top (well, "unreasonable" from the standpoint of more adult fiction – perfectly reasonable for children's). Look at the first book in the series: how Harry has been living in a tiny cupboard under the stairs when we first meet him, the lengths to which his uncle goes to keep Harry from receiving his invitation to Hogwarts, or how the best traps that the top professors could come up with to protect the Sorcerer's (or Philosopher's, if you prefer — not that I, as an American, have any idea what that is, apparently) Stone are ones that could conveniently be bypassed by 11-year-olds. That's not a slam against the first book by any means – children's fiction can (and possibly should) be over-the-top. The problem comes in when grey areas are added. If you are not going to be as over-the-top, then you need to be not over-the-top. Mixing some grey areas with the black/white caricatures just results in the mess known as Book 5.

Look at the character of Umbridge, as an example. She is ridiculously exaggerated as a villain, getting away with much more than she should be able to (how does she cancel the entire Quidditch season? As big as Quidditch apparently is, wouldn't the entirety of the alumni of Hogwarts object?), which — had she been introduced in the first or second books — would have fit. By Book 5, however, when the series has supposedly turned more adult with more grey areas, this caricature of evilness just seems quite out of place. Obviously (and disturbingly) so, in my opinion.

But it is not just the over-the-top-ness portion of this mix that doesn't quite work. Take Harry's father. As the series progresses, Harry continually learns the ways that his father wasn't perfect. Okay, fine, learning one's parents aren't perfect is part of growing up. The problem is how it is handled. I never felt like there was a good reason for this. Is it just to help Harry grow up? Possibly, but why not then give some good along with the bad – as the series progresses, Harry doesn't really gain any new insights or stories about good things his Dad did, just how he mistreated Snape in school. So, was the reason to give backstory and motivation for Snape? Possibly, but as we learn, his motivation was more about Harry's mom than his dad. It really just boiled down to "Dude, your Dad was a jerk!" and that was it. An attempt to add some grey that didn't really have any purpose.

And not having a purpose leads me into my next point:

Plots that Don't Make Sense

Some of the plot points of the books make so little sense that it took me out of the story — I was too busy saying "Now wait a minute..." One example would be the Tri (Quad) Wizard tournament from Book 4 (you knew I was getting back to this). So students from two other schools are forced to come to take classes (are they even taking classes?) at Hogwarts just so that one student from each school can participate in this grand challenge that only entails three tasks over the course of the entire school year? And all other students aren't allowed to take part in their normal activities – such as Quidditch – because of this? Really?

Well, that doesn't make much sense, but once again, Book 4 fails to hold a candle to Book 5 in that department (I didn't like Book 5 at all. Could you tell?). In particular, the infamous Prophecy at the center of the entire book (and in some ways, the center of the entire series). The problem is that this prophecy doesn't really mean anything. It essentially says that Voldemort and Harry will fight to the death. Deep, that. So why exactly do Dumbledore and everyone keep that from Harry? Why does it matter so much to make sure Voldemort doesn't hear the end of it? If it's really that big of a deal, why couldn't the good guys destroy the recording held at the Ministry of Magic? The big fight at the end shows that those globes were easily destroyed, and they already had a copy themselves in the form of Dumbledore's memory. The entire conflict of the book could easily have been avoided by one 30-second conversation. The phrase "Gah!" was heard loudly and quite possibly repeatedly upon finishing Book 5.

Another question: At the end of Book 5, doesn't Dumbledore promise not to keep things from Harry anymore? So why does he *immediately* start keeping things from Harry in Book 6 about the Horcruxes? Why drag out that whole plot/discussion throughout the course of the book when he could sit Harry down and explain things in one go?

There are lots o' questions that can be asked such as these. What they all have in common is:

The Writing

I just don't think J.K. Rowling is a good writer. She has a great imagination and sense of whimsy (usually), but being whimsical can't make up for weak writing. Besides the aforementioned plot issues, questionable character decisions, and attempts to transition from children to young adult to adult, other examples of her writing style that just don't work would be the way she handles character deaths. An example: Sirius' death at the end of Book 5. He is stunned and falls through the curtain between life and death? That's it? What could/should have been a dramatic and poignant death (ignoring how ludicrous the plot was that lead to it to begin with – see above) is just plain stupid. I honestly expected Sirius to come back in some form or another by the end of the series, which would have somewhat justified how he "died," but nope, 'twas not to be, and that "death" really was final.

And the dichotomy in how the various deaths in the final book are handled is rather strange. Some have the proper weight (such as Snape's), but others are mentioned almost in passing, enough so that whilst reading it, I didn't even realize the characters were, in fact, killed – Tonks and Lupin, for instance.

One of the overall issues with the writing is Rowling's penchant for going for convenience rather than consistency. She invents new uses for magic to be used in specific instances seemingly without thinking of how that would affect or change the world she's created. An example: how wizards travel. In Book 2, the Floo Network is introduced. Book 3 has the Knight Bus. Book 4 has portkeys. And Book 5 and beyond focus on apparating. Why do these earlier options exist considering these later options (and why, with all these travel possibilities, do students at Hogwarts still travel by train)? I suppose you could try to come up with reasoning behind each, but it just seems like Rowling needed other ideas in later books to fit the plot points she wanted to make — it was purely a matter of convenience.

Another example: the time-travel device that Hermione uses in Book 3. That's some pretty freakin' powerful magic there, and yet it never shows up again in the series despite many instances where the ability to go back in time even an hour would have helped considerably. Why didn't it? Because it was needed for the Book 3 plot but would have interfered with the later plots! Same with the truth serum (veritaserum, I believe it was called) introduced in Book 4. It appears in Book 5, true, but the sheer existence of such a potion seems like it would have made a lot of things in the wizarding world much easier (couldn't it have proven that Sirius was innocent, for instance?) and yet was only used for certain plot points only.

It reminds me of the episode of *The Simpsons* with Lucy Lawless at a Q&A at the comic book store. She is asked all sorts of nitpicky questions from *Xena* fans, and her response is along the lines of "whenever you notice an inconsistency – a wizard did it" which lucky for J.K. Rowling is an eminently usable excuse for lazy writing.

But it's not just the writing, but also:

The Editing

You may have noticed how many of my issues stem from Books 4 and 5 (and past). This, along with the fact that as of Book 4, all the books are significantly longer than the first three, is not coincidental. I first became aware of the *Harry Potter* books after Book 3 came out, which seems to be about the same time as the massive hype machine started running. As such, it seems as if the editors didn't want to tempt driving their new star writer away by daring to actually edit her work. Books 4 and 5 are way too bloated, Book 6 is just all setup for Book 7, and as for the final book itself – well, when you have entire sections about characters aimlessly wandering around wondering what is going on and what they should be doing, well, that's a sign that perhaps the book could use some trimming down.

Bottom line: the *Harry Potter* series is not bad (my esteemed colleague makes some excellent points, particularly about Hermione). It's just not that good, and in no way deserving of the hype and praise it receives. The first three books? Pretty decent. After that? Not so much. But at least the series got kids to read. Yay, reading!

Now they can go and read something worthy.

– K. Burtt, 2010

-:--:--:--:--:- *GS* -:--:--:--:--:-

Harry Potter: Over-Rated but Still Very, Very Good by B. C. Roberts

Writing about *Harry Potter* is a daunting task. So much has been written already both in support and against. For every person who loved the novels and the world they created, there are just as many (just like my colleague who opposes me in this argument) who find the series over-rated. But despite all this, let's wade once again into the mire that is writing about *Harry Potter*.

First things first. *Of course Harry Potter* is over-rated. This has nothing at all to do with the series itself and everything to do with the hype surrounding it. It is a publishing house's job to create publicity around a product, and just like everything else in the history of marketing, there was some exaggeration (no, Coca Cola will not make you cooler). So claiming that *Harry Potter* doesn't live up to the hype is a non-argument – it can't, the second coming of Christ couldn't.

So the question is really whether or not *Harry Potter* the series is any good at all – or more specifically, does the good outweigh the bad. And I think the answer to this is very strongly in the affirmative.

Let's start with Harry Potter as a character. Harry is not the most gifted wizard, but he is the guy who comes through in a pinch. When it's balls to the wall, Harry time and time again finds a way to survive. He's often lucky — and he always has excellent support — but at the end of the day Harry has that unshakeable self-belief and determination which is common to all great heroes. He isn't the Spider-Man "sit around and feel sorry for myself" type; he's the Batman "use any trick that works" type. And with that comes a fair amount of hubris. When Harry gets thrown into the Tri-Wizard Tournament and doesn't try very hard, it's because he's Harry Fucking Potter, doesn't everyone remember that he killed a basilisk with a sword? And this is one response I find entirely credible. At the age of ten Harry is thrown into a world where he's Jesus Christ, where he is, really, more important than those around him. Now, when sportspeople are put in that position they become self-centered arrogant twits (hello, Tiger), and across the fourth and fifth books Harry does the same. It's hard not to be a narcissist when everyone tells you every single day that you're better than everyone else. But it never gets out of control. His crush on Cho and his awkwardness with her is the perfect example of this.

Then there are the support characters. There are so many amazing characters in this series that it's near impossible to select just a few for special mention. The standout, though, is Hermione Granger. More than anyone else in the entire series, Hermione really demonstrates the possibilities of magic and how incongruous that is with the Muggle world. Hermione begins the series with large buck teeth despite her parents being Muggle dentists, but after Draco Malfoy curses her and makes the teeth grow longer and longer, Hermione has Madame Pomfrey shrink the teeth down to a normal size. Her parents would be horrified. Hermione's shining moment for me, though, comes in the final book. Everyone important is at the Weasley's house for Bill and Fleur's wedding when Death Eaters attack and everyone scatters. Hermione disapparates with Ron and Harry, the two boys have nothing with them but the clothes on their backs, and they wonder how they will get back to the Burrow to collect everything they need for the quest ahead:

> *"Undetectable Extension Charm," said Hermione.*
> *"Tricky but I think I've done it OK; anyway, I*
> *managed to fit everything we need in here." She gave*
> *the fragile-looking bag a little shake and it echoed like*
> *a cargo hold as a number of heavy objects rolled*
> *around inside it. "Oh damn, that'll be the books," she*
> *said, peering into it, "and I had them all stacked by*
> *subject..."*

It's brilliant and so is Hermione. Sure, Harry's name is the one of the front of the book, but Hermione's awesomeness is hardly an argument against the greatness of the series. The same goes for all the other marvelous support characters. From Hagrid to Professor Trelawney, Grawp to (my personal favorite) Gilderoy Lockhart. They are all masterful creations, each believable within the logic of the series, always hitting just the right level of strange and extraordinary, but also with real world counterparts.

But far and away the shining achievement of the *Harry Potter* series is the creation of the perfect fantasy world. For every child who reads that first book, when Hagrid breaks into a far-flung shack on a rocky island and tells Harry that he's a wizard, there's the same excitement that magic could one day appear in their world and spirit them off to the most wondrous of schools. Harry's world is so close to ours that the possibility of the one spilling into the other is always tantalizing.

The most impressive thing about Hogwarts and *Harry Potter*'s entire magical world is the way it blends the real world into the imaginary. It isn't just that Hogwarts is the most exciting place to go to school on the planet or that flying on a broom and repeatedly saving the wizarding world (sometime around the end of each school year) is fantastic, but rather that it all seems so possible and well, so British. It seems, in the context of the novels, perfectly obvious that British wizards would drink cups of tea and eat bread-and-butter pudding. They could have the house elves prepare anything in the world, real or imaginary, but they stick to what is widely recognized as one of the worst cuisines in the world. God love 'em.

Sure, the novels go from being simple children's fiction to more dramatic young teen fare and along the way things get longer and darker, but the consistency throughout the series is not lost. The blend of crazy and mundane stays well balanced and I particularly love the wizarding version of a police state that we get towards the end of the series. Umbridge, for example, is at once surprising in her cruel punishments and penchant for pink and at the same time entirely predictable as the archetype of the government agent who takes her job too far and too seriously. At every stage she is an imaginative creation and a carbon copy of South American fascists.

No writer in any genre has managed to create such a complete, coherent and compelling world. The rules of magic are set out very early on and consistently applied (unlike the disaster that is the His Dark Materials series) and we are never provided with random new rules that we are just expected to accept (à la Artemis Fowl). The wizarding world is at all times simultaneously fantastic and completely believable, and that is a feat not to be sneezed at.

– B. C. Roberts, 2010

Love in SFF: Awesome Women Falling for Losers by B. C. Roberts

Love stories are a staple of any genre and have been a mainstay of literature for as long as people have been writing, or even when they were still reciting the latest in epic poetry in classical Greece. But it seems that today in Science Fiction and Fantasy (SFF) there is a real surplus of what I am going to call "touching love stories." These are the ones where the two lovers must conquer some great obstacle in order to be together and that having conquered that obstacle things turn out perfectly romantically (which either means everyone dies, a la *Romeo and Juliet*, or they live happily ever after, a la *Much Ado About Nothing*).

There are no two stories in SFF bigger right now than Harry Potter and *Twilight*. But I'm going to ignore them both. It's just too easy to complain about the monstrous stupidity and offensive sexism (not to mention ludicrous celibacy) of the relationships in *Twilight*. Similarly, complaining that Hermione falling for Ron is like *Nikita*'s eponymous heroine falling in love with Nameless Henchman Number 4, or *Chuck*'s Sarah going for Morgan, is just too obvious. So instead I want to talk about *Avatar, Underworld, The Fifth Element* and, pushing the boundaries of what counts as genre, *Salt*.

The theme in all these movies is that a strong, fabulous, independent woman falls in love with some type of loser, and this incredibly unlikely love interest is either used to drive the action or resolve the major conflict. But it's not just that I object to awesome women falling for losers. We've all seen it and at some point you either get really bitter or you learn to live with it (or you use it to your advantage... but I wouldn't know anything that). It's that basing a movie on an unrealistic love story does more to make a movie feel unrealistic than Ben-Hur wearing a wristwatch. As much as we all love to see humans flying through space or weaving magic in castles, there is a base expectation that humans continue to act relatively consistently with how they act now. This is the complex counter-factual at the heart of all genre: "If I was a starship commander would I have sex with every hot alien I met?" The answer is "Hell yes!," and therein lies the inherent believability of the greatest space sleaze of them all, James T. Kirk. But consider the opposite side of the equation: "'Would I, as a woman/hot female alien, who is otherwise strong, independent and has the respect of my people, fall for an outsider who can bring me only trouble and a strange-looking human/alien hybrid baby thing?" I don't think the answer to that is so unequivocal. Hence, if you expect the audience to buy the fact that someone with everything to lose from a relationship is nevertheless going to throw herself, blue booty and all, right into it, you really have to convince us.

So let's look at the motivation for Neytiri (Zoe Saldana), the main blue character in 2009's *Avatar*, falling in love with Jake Sully (Sam Worthington), poster boy for advocacy group "The disabled can land hot chicks too, but only if they're another species" (look them up). Neytiri knows that Jake is an outsider and allied with the people who are destroying the rest of her planet. But, through the magic of the montage, the two spend enough time together to fall madly in love, mainly because Jake is basically proficient at being a Na'vi. What about all the Na'vi who are awesome at being Na'vi? Surely that's hotter than an outsider just being okay at it? Of course she falls in love before Jake tames that really big flying thing and proves to be a great Na'vi. Are we supposed to assume that she could see within him all along and knew that he would be great? Is that something we really believe? Every woman I have ever met who has been convinced that she sees within her loser boyfriend the prospect of greatness ends up being sorely disappointed. So does Neytiri forget he's one of the humans? Or that the other humans have been largely banned from the tribe?

Maybe I'm just failing to appreciate the awesome power of the montage.

The other major problem is SFF is that with all the effort being put into the creation of an interesting alternative world, the love of the central characters is simply taken for granted without any real explanation. In 2003's *Underworld*, for example, Selene (Kate Beckinsale), who has spurned the advances of every other vampire for centuries, falls for a human who has been bitten by a werewolf. Being bitten means that the human, Michael (Scott Speedman), will inevitably turn into a werewolf—the very creatures that Selene has devoted her life to wiping out. More than any other vampire, Selene hates the werewolves, but is willing to risk it all for this human. Sure, he turns out to have the potential to turn into some super-cool vampire/werewolf hybrid, but Selene's in love before she knows any of that. So what are we meant to believe, that deep within a hundreds-year-old vampyre there lurks a winsome girl just longing for the right man to come along? The love story here is jarring, not because *Underworld* is a bad movie (as my opponent hurtfully claims) but rather because it is otherwise a very good SFF movie. The motivation of every other character is clear, the motivations of Selene in every other respect are clear. But what we get at the center of the movie is a love story that is there just because love stories are supposed to be there.

Which brings us to *The Fifth Element* (1997), a truly classic SFF movie in which Bruce Willis again proves that among all the 80s action heroes, he's the only one who can step outside his core genre and pull it off. Again, the central love story is one of opposites attracting. Korben Dallas (Willis) is ex-Special Ops, now driving/flying a taxi. One day, through the sort of luck one would only find on the screen, damsel in distress Leeloo falls through the roof of his cab. It's kind of an "of all the taxicabs, in all the cities in all the world…" moment. From then on Dallas goes to great lengths to help Leeloo save the world, his prime motivation being that she's hot. And let's be honest. It's Milla Jovovich at her best; who wouldn't fight a few aliens to tap that? Where it all gets a bit unbelievable is when Leeloo, having experienced the worst that the universe has to offer in terms of evil people trying to kill her, and having learnt all about the atrocities of the 20th century (in the future, computers only show history up until the turn of the millennium) Leeloo has to make the choice between letting humanity rot and saving every rotten one of them. And what is the defining moment in her choice? It's that the love of Bruce Willis is more profound than World Wars and a variety of genocides. Really? Won't somebody please make a movie where humanity is damned, love isn't enough to overcome evil, and everyone dies?

And finally, just a quick word about *Salt*, a 2010 movie I've only just seen. Angelina Jolie plays Evelyn Salt, a Russian sleeper agent who is activated and told to kill the Russian President. Evelyn is married to a German arachnologist, Krause (August Diehl), who was an asset she seduced in order to get access to North Korea. She falls for him and agrees to marry him when he campaigns for her release from North Korean prison (where she was being horribly tortured), after both the CIA and KGB leave her for dead. So, just for a change, here is a pretty believable reason to fall in love with someone. For some reason I haven't been able to fathom, though, marrying Krause makes her side with America rather than Russia. Long before the Russians kill Krause (at which point her loyalty to America is assured), Evelyn decides to disobey her Russian handlers and not to kill the Russian President. The audience is expected to accept that love explains all decisions, even when it explains none, or at least not why one choice would be made over another equal one. If anyone has a good answer for this, please e-mail me.

I have now had the opportunity to read the hugely entertaining opposing piece for this month, and I agree completely with our Rachel Day that a good love story can make an average movie into a great one. I have my doubts about whether *The Mummy* falls into that category, but nonetheless I take her point. For her few examples, though, the weight of unbelievable, poorly-conceived, poorly-detailed love stories in SFF clearly falls to my side. Sure, love stories can be moving but, as my counterpart points out, love stories get put into every genre as a matter of course. And oftentimes, rather than driving the action or drawing the audience in, they're just stupid.

– *B. C. Roberts, 2011*

-:--:--:--:--:- *GS* -:--:--:--:--:-

Love in SFF: Love is a Vital Element by Rachel Day

Needless to say, I'm going to have to respectfully disagree with my colleague's erstwhile argument that there are too many "touching love stories" in the SFF genre. Love is a vital element within genre because well-drawn believable characters have relationships with others that resonate with and draw an audience into the story, and that's not going to change any time soon. Where would the world of sci-fi and fantasy be without Han and Leia, Bella and Edward, or Kirk and Spock? (OK, so maybe I made the last one up, but that relationship is a serious bromance by anyone's standard).

The problem, B. C. argues, is too many "touching love stories" which focus on soul-mates overcoming epic obstacles on a journey of destiny to be together; to which I reply: well, it never harmed the popularity of Shakespeare's *Romeo and Juliet* any – or to make this genre, the popularity of Mercedes Lackey's Valdemar series. Indeed, a good love story can make even the crappiest film, TV show or book of any genre better, and a great love story can make it popular beyond the wildest dreams of its creators. There's a reason why romance is the best-selling genre of published fiction; why shipping (the active fan support for a particular relationship) is such a widespread fandom activity; why film producers insist on including a romance sub-plot into all genres that aren't romance itself. Love equals money in the business of books, film and television.

But let's talk some specifics: my colleague isn't going to tackle Harry Potter and *Twilight*, and neither will I. Primarily because I would argue that Hermione ending up with Ron is nothing but a contrivance to ensure Harry ended up with someone else and its only obstacle being Ron acting like a prat. And as much as I enjoyed the *Twilight* series, I still deplore Bella changing herself to be with Edward (possibly I'm wearing my Team Jacob t-shirt right now).

However, neither am I going to talk about the films that my colleague covers because; firstly, what's the fun in that?; and secondly, with the exception of *The Fifth Element* I haven't actually seen them. Yes, yes, I will get around to watching *Avatar* one day, but why anyone would willingly watch *Underworld* or *Salt* is something of a mystery to me. *[You MUST watch* Underworld *immediately! – Ed.]* Except to say that while I do have my own issues with *The Fifth Element* – Korben Dallas (Bruce Willis) being revealed as ex-Special Ops being one of them, (like the leading man having a crack military background isn't an over-used trope in the genre at all) – I have no issues with the improbable love story in what is ultimately a camp not-to-be-taken-seriously movie. Boy meets girl. Boy falls in love with girl. Boy finds out girl is an artificially created life form meant to save the world. Girl saves the day with the Power of Their Love. What's the problem?

Since my opponent chose four films to illustrate his point, then so too will I: the *Star Wars* saga, *WALL-E*, *Batman Returns*, and *The Mummy*. All four are wildly different, hugely successful and yet have at their heart a "touching love story."

The Mummy actually has two "touching love stories" at its heart: one in the shape of the relationship between American hero Rick (Brendan Fraser) and ditzy but incredibly smart Evelyn (Rachel Weisz), and one in the history of Imhotep (Arnold Vosloo) and Anck-Su-Namun (Patricia Velásquez). Both face epic obstacles and have a destined love. The latter is a tragedy with two corrupt lovers; the former, a happy-ending fairy tale for opposites who attract. Both are integral to the plot, to the characters' motivations, to providing angst and tension in amongst the action sequences. Both give the movie some depth beyond an enjoyable romp. *The Mummy* would be nothing without its touching love stories.

The same goes for *WALL-E*. Yes, it is an animated film but it's robots in space with an apocalyptic Earth. Regardless of the environmental and dieting messages embedded in the movie, the heart of it is the "touching love story" between WALL-E and EVE. They meet and face epic obstacles, but eventually get their happily ever after. I cried. I'm not ashamed to admit it. OK, maybe a little ashamed, because they are at the end of the day animated robots, but seriously, the scene where EVE fixes WALL-E and he doesn't remember her? I'm welling up just thinking about it. Their love gives the movie emotion and drama; it elevates the fairly twee plot and makes me want to hug an automaton of some kind.

Obviously, I'd much prefer to be hugging Han Solo. Ah, the epic love of Han and Leia, which survived getting captured by the Empire, Han being frozen in carbonite and Leia almost falling out of her gold bikini. Where would the original *Star Wars* trilogy be without the sub-plot of Han and Leia's "touching love story" — and the admittedly slightly icky triangle when Luke turns out to be Leia's brother?

The best of the shaky prequels (and what saved them from being complete tripe in my opinion) is the romantic tragedy of Anakin and Padme. Their forbidden love and the desperation of Anakin (Hayden Christensen) in wanting to save Padme (Natalie Portman) enabling his fall to the Dark Side, only for his fall to be the catalyst for her death, is actually heart-tugging. It makes the eventual redemption of Darth Vader/Anakin in the saga even more poignant.

Poignant and tragic are also words to describe the "touching love story" between Catwoman (Michelle Pfeiffer) and Batman (Michael Keaton) in the fabulous *Batman Returns*. It is often heralded as the best of the Batman movies, and I would argue the reason for that is the incredible relationship that evolves between these characters. I love that final scene in the Penguin's lair when she kills Shreck (Christopher Walken); the desperation of Batman in revealing his own identity in trying to reach out to her, her wanting to give into him but ultimately refusing to trust him and deny her nature. TRAGIC!! (Yes, the caps lock is necessary.)

The common element in all these films is that the "touching love story" is believable on some level. And while I admit some of the genre romances out there leave a lot to be desired in terms of believability and are just badly drawn, badly written and badly executed, the SFF genre as a whole would be a much poorer place without the touching love stories that are great; that pull at the audience's emotions and make us cry; that provide a window into humanity that we can relate to in stories that otherwise present us with strange new worlds. If for every *Underworld*, I get a *Batman Returns* – well, I can live with that.

– *Rachel Day, 2011*

-:--:--:--:--:- *GS* -:--:--:--:--:-

Rewatching TV: A Waste of Precious Time by B. C. Roberts

Once upon a time there was a TV show called *Buffy the Vampire Slayer*. You might have heard of it. For seven seasons it consumed the *otaku* of the western world with its edgy take on adolescence and its super-hot titular character. Well, actually, it consumed us for three seasons and then it got a bit disappointing but we all kept watching thinking it would get better until finally we couldn't explain why we kept watching since it clearly wasn't.

Now, I particularly really liked the third season of *Buffy,* and recently a friend gave me a copy of it. Not on DVD of course, because I am morally opposed to purchasing something when it can be obtained for free. Anyway, I dutifully copied this season onto my hard drive and looked at it briefly before... I went off to watch something I hadn't seen before.

Without being too philosophical, our time on this earth is relatively brief. We only get eighty or so years to experience everything that art and literature have managed to produce in the last twenty-three centuries. The odds are stacked against anyone getting even close to just keeping up with all the new shows that go to air every week, let alone going back to the classics. Do we really have time to re-watch Buffy angst over Angel after he comes back from Hell? Or Xander and Cordelia to-ing and fro-ing about getting together and then Xander getting busted making out with Willow and so on and so forth? When I haven't even finished reading *War and Peace* yet? Or, to be less pretentious, when I have never even watched *Alias*? There is always something new to experience, something that has the potential to add to me as a human being. Watching something I have already seen can never achieve that – I have already seen it, I already know what's going to happen.

That being said, I also oppose going back to watch a show that I missed when it aired that is anything less than an absolute classic. What would I gain from going back to watch triple (or was it quintuple?) agent Sydney Bristow and the various stuff she did which was no doubt a bit sexy (though less sexy than just watching porn) and full of action (though less action than watching an early Jackie Chan movie)? The answer, I am afraid, is absolutely nothing. Whatever would be the point? There are hundreds of shows soon to air as the ratings season starts back in the US and I have no chance of keeping up with them. I will struggle to fit more than a few into my life as it is, why would I go back and watch something (and watch out for the key word here) OLD?

Because ultimately, I think this is the problem. Stuff that is old is automatically less interesting than stuff that is new. Why is this? Because watching something old is, always in some respect, an act of nostalgia. And nostalgia is the single most pointless of human self-indulgences. I could be watching Season 3 of *Buffy* right now thinking about who I was then and how I have changed in the intervening decade and you know what? I would gain absolutely nothing from the process. For two main reasons. First is that nothing about re-watching a show can change how I was then and reflection on who I am now is mostly aided by my reaction to the new. Second is that Joss Whedon is not Aristotle or James Joyce. Close re-reading of his texts do not reveal a nuanced and insightful commentary on human nature—his work is not the study of fields like philosophy or social theory. Study of Whedon is relegated to the "mongrel domain" of cultural studies (to quote Pierre Bourdieu), which has made an academic discipline of everything. Thus studies of *Buffy* detailing "depictions of teenagers in 90s pop culture" are a far cry from studies of social justice or philosophical meaning.

This is not to say that one should prohibited from engaging with popular culture. There are even some movies I like enough that I have seen them three or four times. But if a person chooses to re-watch a television season of somewhere between 12 and 24 episodes, they cannot pretend that doing so is akin to re-reading the *Nicomachean Ethics*. And if it is not a study, then what does re-watching amount to? In short, a waste of precious time. Time which could be spent learning or watching something new. Being human is a restless search for the novel, the undiscovered. Re-watching TV is its antithesis. Re-watching a TV show treats life like an endless expanse of time to kill; as if there is nothing better to do than wait for your life to slowly end.

Soon enough we will all be dust and our beloved, oft-watched boxed set of *Firefly* is going to be sitting forlorn in the $3 bin of a second-hand shop. And every hour we wasted re-watching that episode where we almost thought that Mal and Inara were going to kiss is an hour less we were doing anything even remotely worthwhile, useful or… gasp!… entertaining.

– *B. C. Roberts, 2011*

-:--:--:--:--:- *GS* -:--:--:--:--:-

Rewatching TV: Finding Your Happy Place by Geonn Cannon

Nostalgia is dumb. Why bother looking back when there are new and exciting experiences happening right in front of you? So don't buy TV shows on DVD. Also, throw out your wedding album, trash that high school yearbook, and tape over those old home movies (but not with TV shows). My esteemed colleague believes there are far too few minutes on this Earth to "waste" it re-watching a TV show. I respectfully disagree. Yes, every fall I have a minor panic attack when I think about all the new shows coming on and the precious amount of time I have to watch all that I want. But just because there's a new crop of shows doesn't mean you have to turn your back on the favorites of yesteryear.

The first show I actively collected on DVD was *Stargate SG-1*, because it was not only my favorite show, but I honestly believe it changed my life. At the beginning of their eighth season, I embarked on a trip to a convention. My first convention, my first trip out of state (and out of the country). It was really my first time away from home in a new environment where I wasn't my parents' kid or my brother's brother. I was just me, with nothing but myself to rely on, and it was immensely freeing. What going to college must have felt like to smart people. While there, I took a brief side-trip to a small island that sparked an idea, which grew into a story, which became my first published novel.

Stargate SG-1 REALLY meant something to me. The characters and the stories were like old friends, and some days I just long to revisit them. It doesn't matter that I can quote lines, it doesn't matter that I know exactly how Sam Carter is going to save the day or that I know Daniel Jackson really is going to die this time (no matter how briefly). What matters is revisiting that world and seeing the characters you fell in love with. Watching one episode can remind you of the years you spent carving out an hour of your Friday night to take another trip through the Stargate.

We don't have perfect recall. Like my colleague says, there are so many new shows coming out that eventually even my quotable knowledge of *Stargate* begins to fade. I'll forget a favorite joke. I'll be fuzzy on the details. So maybe I'll go back and find an episode that isn't quite so clear in my mind and I'll take a refresher course, and it's almost like watching it again for the first time. An episode that I wasn't completely in love with the first time takes on a whole new life on DVD.

When you're watching a show you love week-to-week, you're a slave to the schedule. If a bad episode comes along, or if it just focuses on a character that's not your favorite, then that's your fix for the week, like it or lump it. But on DVD, that episode is just one of twenty or so. You give it a bit more leeway. And maybe, just maybe, you'll realize that you didn't give it a real chance.

The main argument against rewatching TV shows seems to be "You've already seen this, what's the point?" But it's not rational, it's love. It's comfort food. Sure, the upcoming show *Person of Interest* looks exciting, but so did *Undercovers*. Sometimes you want to watch a show where you know the good guys win and have fantastic snark while doing it. Favorite TV shows are like a comfy sweatshirt. It just makes you feel good to have it back. You know how the *Leverage* team will pull off their con, but that doesn't make it any less exciting to watch them put it together. In some ways, it's even better because you are actually in on the con this time around. You can see all the little traps and pitfalls that you (and the bad guy) overlooked the first time.

Which brings me to my next point: spoilers don't spoil. There was recently a new study that revealed people enjoy a story more when they know how it will end. When you're watching something for the first time, you're anxious. Knowing how it will all turn out relaxes you and allows you to fully enjoy the ride. I may not fully support that theory for first-time viewings, (spoil me for *Sanctuary* and you die, simple as that) but it definitely holds up for repeat viewings. You can relax and get into the story, and that's why people buy TV shows on DVD. It's why people buy books, for the inevitable re-read where they can focus on the story a bit more. The first time through, you're building the house. The second time through, you get to appreciate all the small touches and accents. And these days, with shows becoming more friendly to season-long arcs, you can watch it all from the beginning and pick up the clues you missed the first time around. Shows like *Lost* almost demand rewatching the entire series every now and again.

And the best thing about not only watching but owning your favorite TV shows is converting friends. Maybe one of my friends never saw *Better Off Ted* just because of crappy scheduling or bad advertising (I watched the darn show, and even I'm not sure what day it aired). But I saw it, and I loved it, and I bought the DVD set as soon as I could. And maybe one of your friends sees the set on your shelf, or maybe they realize you're watching a show that barely limped through two seasons before getting axed, and they decide to give it a shot. And now it's shiny and new to them.

I'm not saying run out and buy every season of every show you like. I love *The Office,* but it's on cable way more than enough for you to get your fix. But what about shows that aren't being repeated? I used to love *The Invisible Man* on Sci-Fi, but it's never shown. I recently got the DVDs and I'm falling in love with it all over again. Ten years on, I've forgotten a good chunk of what happened on that show. That's why I'm so eager for a *Terriers* release. That show will never be reaired in syndication, and I'm worried one day it won't even be found on the interwebs. Sometimes shows just disappear, and DVDs are a safeguard, promising you'll always be able to find that one episode of that one show you truly loved even if no one else even remembers it.

Sometimes when you buy a TV show on DVD, the episodes are almost like a bonus feature. Maybe you're really buying the commentary, or the behind-the-scenes footage. Maybe the actors and writers went to the trouble of making original webisodes that you can see for the first time in all their glory.

And leaving one of the most important points for last... making a TV show is expensive. Watching on the interwebs for free is fine, but it does nothing for the cast and crew, and it gives the studio very little incentive to keep the show around. When I really love a show, I have no problem shelling out forty or fifty dollars so I can have the show I love while at the same time giving them a little money to keep the show on the air. If you think DVD sales don't matter, watch the latest new episode of *Family Guy* or *Futurama* and get back to me.

I'm not including the benefits of watching on DVD versus watching live – no insanely irritating bugs in the corner (I don't

WANT to watch *Ghost Hunters International*, so stop covering up a quarter of the show I DO want to see with those pop-ups), no commercials – because that's not the issue. The issue is shelling out your hard-earned money for a show you've already watched.

I take pride in the fact that I've seen every episode of *Stargate SG-1* at least five times. I can quote Aldo Raine's full speech from his first scene of *Inglourious Basterds* ("My name is Lieutenant Aldo Raine, and I'm putting together a special team and I need me eight soldiers. Eight. Jewish. Am'rican soldiers.").

New is great. New is exciting. What's old to one person may be new to someone else. I'm just getting into the original UK version of *Life on Mars*, and I'm doing it on DVD. But just because something is new doesn't make it inherently better than something you've already seen. I'll take the pilot of *Lost* over any single episode of *Undercovers*. We revisit the things we love. We refresh our memories of characters, stories, quotes because sometimes life is long. Life is busy. And we need to turn the page back and think, "Oh, yeah, *that's* why I love Sam Carter."

No one can buy every single show they like on DVD, it's just not feasible. But the shows you love, the shows that in five years you may have an itch to see one more time... those are the shows that are worth paying a little money for, just so you'll always have it.

Shh, shh, hold on... this is my favorite part.

– Geonn Cannon, 2011

-:--:--:--:--:- *GS* -:--:--:--:--:-

Superpowers: Why I'd Be a Superhero, or How Could Anyone Even Contemplate Being Anything Else? by Rachel Hyland

Did you know that there are people who, if gifted with superpowers in some way or another (radioactive spider bite, doused with radioactive chemicals, exposed to radioactive isotopes... really, comic land would be nothing without nuclear physics), would choose to use those powers not for good but for evil? That there are those who, when immersed in a hypothetical discussion regarding said powers, deny any wish to don a mask and/or a cape to save their fellow man from miscreants and ne'er do wells, but instead would use those powers to rob banks and create havoc and generally be the dark nemeses against which all our favorite secret-identitied, selfless vigilantes so valiantly campaign?

I suppose I always knew this intellectually, on some level. The sad fact is that there are people of questionable moral fiber in the world, a reality we are confronted with every night on the news: thieves and murderers, warlords and dictators, everywhere lawbreakers just as merciless and as egocentric as even the most maniacal of fictional criminal masterminds. It stands to reason, then, that those kinds of people would be quite taken with the notion of possessing superpowers, if only to enhance their own prestige and make the subjugation of others less bothersome. But that someone I *know* should hold this opinion; and someone, moreover, that I would have no hesitation in characterizing as one of my very best friends… Well, let's just say, that came as something of a shock.

Do otherwise good, decent, thoughtful people *really* want to be the bad guy?

Oh, it's not that I don't understand the allure of the dark side. Ruthless Darth Vader is cooler than the whiny, sappy Anakin; unrepentant Angelus is funnier than the tortured, brooding Angel; mischievous Catwoman is sexier than the terribly earnest Batgirl. But it is one thing to find assorted villains captivating and quite another to want to *be* one of them; it's the difference between playing *Grand Theft Auto* and running down sex workers and assorted pedestrians in stolen cars and actually running down sex workers and assorted pedestrians in stolen cars. The former might be an enjoyable way to kill time living faux dangerously (or so I hear), but the latter is an anti-social lifestyle choice that can only reveal one as a homicidal psychopath unsuited to polite society.

So the fact that any fine, upstanding citizen would proclaim their desire to become a supervillain instead of a superhero, should the occasion ever arise, just doesn't make sense to me — especially a fine, upstanding citizen who, I break no confidences in revealing, has a tattoo of Spider-Man secreted somewhere about his person. If supervillains are so utterly superior, why didn't my colleague's reckless younger self have the Green Goblin indelibly marked on his body? Or Doctor Octopus? Or Kangaroo? (Okay, I get why not Kangaroo… a dude who can just jump kind of high against a guy who can swing through the city and crawl up buildings? Worst Spidey villain ever.)

Now, further discussion of the issue revealed that when he said supervillain, what my formidable opponent actually thought he meant was super-anti-hero; he wanted to use his newfound theoretical strength to cripple irresponsible energy companies and the avaricious financial sector and rid us all of the menace of international copyright law. But the difference between an anti-hero and a villain – and especially a supervillain – lies not in their intent but in their utter lack of conscience, and given that the collateral damage such a campaign of anti-trust terror must necessarily engender bothered my adversary not at all, I would suggest that "supervillain" was indeed the correct nomenclature.

It could be said (and was said, also by my opponent in this debate) that superheroes operate outside the law as much as do villains, and as such it is difficult to differentiate between them in mere words; we simply know them when we see them. I disagree—I think the main distinction lies in one word: sacrifice. A superhero will sacrifice himself for any random other with barely a moment's thought, but it is the rare supervillain who will endanger his own life/liberty/pursuit of happiness in favor of even a loved one, let alone a stranger dangling precariously from a collapsed bridge. (Which he probably collapsed in the first place.)

Sure, superheroes may, like their villainous counterparts, often do the wrong thing for what they perceive to be the right reasons, and they are just as often hunted by assorted law enforcement agencies as are their own dangerous prey – from Batman to The Punisher to Deadpool (only one of whom is usually depicted with actual superpowers, by the by), these heroes can be, and are, just as easily painted as villains. But despite their often dubious methods, each would without hesitation lay down their lives to Do the Right Thing; it's doubtful the same could be said of any incarnation of The Joker, or Jigsaw, or… who the hell is Deadpool's archenemy, anyway? T-Ray? He has so many.

The simple fact is, a superhero – however reluctantly – feels he or she must save the world, while a supervillain merely wants to take it over, and then make it over in his or her own image. As Dr. Horrible put it so concisely: "The world is a mess, and I just need to... rule it." That is very much at the core of the supervillain credo. The difference between Professor X and Magneto is not in their ideas – they both want mutants to be safe and accepted by the population at large – but in how they choose to achieve their ends. The one campaigns for slow, steady change, ultimately bringing mutant and human together as one, with the strong protecting the weak for the good of all; the other wants to assert his own dominion, sure that mutants are a superior species and should therefore take their rightful place as humanity's lords and masters.

When Superman collected up all the planet's nuclear weapons and sent them into the sun in *Superman IV: The Quest for Peace*, it was an act of villainy, because not only did it give Lex Luthor the opportunity to – somewhat farfetchedly – make his own super being to do battle with poor Supes, but it took away humanity's right to make our own mistakes, imposing his Kryptonian will on ours just because he could. When, at the end of the movie, he realized that universal nuclear disarmament was a matter to be decided by nations and not by one man, he was returned to his superhero status. A superhero can make mistakes, but he acknowledges them, learns from them, is humbled by them—and often dwells on them ad infinitum until we're all ready to scream at them: "Dude, okay, you got your uncle killed, like fifty years ago, get over it." A superhero will blame himself; a supervillain will blame everyone else. Another key difference.

But to return to Superman's usurpation of the UN and his grand larceny of WMDs: when my opponent says he would use his theoretical superpowers to destabilize our banking systems and rid the world of fossil fuels and who knows what anarchistic else, what he's really saying is he believes it is one man's prerogative to determine the course of all human history based solely on his own beliefs and doctrines, and he would impose his will on us all at the point of a laser eyebeam; might equals right. He doesn't seek to save or protect on the micro level, as might, say, Daredevil stop a mugging or Wonder Woman thwart a kidnapping or The Authority prevent a planetary invasion by, uh, God. Instead, he seeks to compel obedience to his whims on a worldwide scale; the very hallmark of a supervillain.

Also, from a purely practical standpoint, deciding to be a supervillain is just pretty foolish, because eventually you will be brought to justice, though it may take decades worth of comics – or an entire movie – to do it, and even then you'll probably escape from jail or be brought back from the dead because, hey, every hero needs his nemesis. And admittedly, a superhero's lot is not always a happy one, always hiding your good deeds and staying one step ahead of the conventional law and not really getting to have henchmen. Henchmen would be fun.

Perhaps when it comes right down to it, being a superhero is less appealing than being the opposite, and I admit here and now, I would probably suck at it. Forget joining The Avengers or any of the X teams, I don't think I'd even make the grade as one of the Mystery Men, and one of their members' only power is being invisible when no one is looking at him. But the alternative just doesn't bear thinking about. To quote Churchill: "No one pretends that democracy is perfect or all-wise. Indeed, it has been said that democracy is the worst form of government except all those other forms that have been tried from time to time." No one pretends a superhero is perfect or all-wise, and certainly being a superhero would have its challenges, and more than its share of frustrations. But to do anything else? To ignore your great responsibility when great power is thrust upon you, and instead become an egomaniacal, megalomaniacal madman letting power corrupt absolutely and intent on world domination, no matter how ostensibly noble the goals?

No. Hell, no. If for no other reason than the seemingly mandatory evil laughs have become just so passé.

– *Rachel Hyland, 2017*

-:--:--:--:--:- *GS* -:--:--:--:--:-

Superpowers: Why I'd Be a Supervillain, or There Are Only Superheroes Because They Don't Think Big Enough by B. C. Roberts

Right now there are over a billion people in the world living on less than US$2 a day. Starvation kills hundreds of people every day. Lack of clean drinking water is responsible for at least 30,000 deaths every day. At the same time there are more people in the world who are overweight than there are people who are starving. And the fortunes of the world's richest one hundred people could lift every single person on the planet out of poverty.

Our illustrious (and virtuous) editor has laid down quite the challenge, arguing forcefully that we should choose heroism over villainy because being a super villain is just so... well... wrong. And she's right.

That's the point.

To start with the persistent argument across all of genre that humanity must be left to make its own mistakes, that every super-powered person who attempts to relieve humanity of this apparently basic human right (though needless to say it doesn't appear in the Universal Declaration of Human Rights or any other such document) is a villain.

In 2012, when Israel and Palestine were blowing each other up and posturing that considerably greater violence was to come, Hilary Clinton and Mohammed Morsi brokered a peace that neither side sought. Israel seemed hell bent on "making its own mistakes" by eradicating Palestine and Hamas was equally committed to "making its own mistakes" by bombing whatever bit of Israel it could direct rockets at. Now, nobody would suggest that Clinton and Morsi's role was anything other than coercive – without the backing of the US and Egypt, Israel and Palestine respectively could not expect to continue existing. And nobody in their right mind would say that this peace deal removed anyone's fundamental rights to anything. The entire international legal machinery is designed to prevent humanity making its worst mistakes.

When Superman destroyed all the nuclear weapons in *Superman IV* (see the opposite argument), he wasn't removing humanity's dubious right to make its own mistakes. He was helping us be the best we can be, rather than defending our worst. The Nuclear Disarmament treaties are the best of humans, but which our corrupt politics is too broken to implement. That is, the international community had already decided nukes should go, they just couldn't make it happen. When Superman decided he was in error he became less than a hero; he became a colluder with all the powerful regimes who use their position to tyrannize the weak.

Was Iron Man being a villain in his first movie outing when he intervened in an international conflict to save the inhabitants of a village? Of course not. We expect superheroes to intervene. And so, if I woke up with superpowers, I'd really really REALLY intervene. And I think it would make me a supervillain in the end.

So if the question is whether I would use super powers to intervene on a global scale and remake the world into something better rather than nab bag snatchers there can only be one answer: get the fuck out of my way.

...

OK. So hopefully you're still reading.

Let's consider how this might work. One day you wake up with the powers of Superman. We'll use Superman because when people talk superheroes he is clearly the paradigm. If you wake up with the powers of Aquaman, fine, be a minor superhero, what are you going to do really?

But you wake up with near absolute invulnerability, super-strength, super-speed, the ability to fly, laser beam eyes, x-ray vision, super strong breath and the ability to effectively disguise yourself by putting on a pair of eyeglasses. You are, in almost every way, superior in abilities to everyone else on the planet.

At first you think that you would like to help some people out. You go to school and save a few kids from being bullied. You cruise around town and stop a few car thieves and muggers. You notice that a lot of your family's friends are having their houses foreclosed upon. Your particular part of small town America has been hard hit by the local auto factory closing down and now everyone is out of work and the banks are moving in. You think, surely, with this near limitless power, I can help out the people in my town.

A few ideas occur to you. You could become a successful MMA fighter though with your strength it would hardly be fair (and potentially lethal) for your opponents. You could hold a benefit, announce your powers to the world, and ask for donations. I guess it could work, but there are a lot of houses to save. You could strong-arm the bank manager and make him back off on the foreclosures. That might work for a little while, but how long could it last?

Or you can steal some money—no, steal a SHITLOAD of money, and make everyone's problems disappear. You could distribute it in small amounts, enough to cover each repayment so that nobody need ever suspect that the lost money from that Argentinian bank heist ended up in Smallville. The criminal option is tantalizing and no matter how hard you try to think about other options you become fixated on how many awful corporations there are making so much money off small-scale tragedies like the one in your town. So you steal the money, everyone is saved, and you go back to local patrol duty, hoping that you haven't permanently tarnished your character.

You finish school and end up in the big city. Every night (apparently never needing to sleep is another of your super powers) you protect the city, but crime seems never ending and the poor just keep getting poorer. One day your best friend comes to you and tells you he has been busted for possessing a small amount of marijuana. Now, you have always supported decriminalization of marijuana and you're pretty angry that poor Jimmy Olsen is facing a stint in prison for smoking weed. You do some research online and discover that America incarcerates a greater proportion of its population than any other country and that the great majority of these are for petty drug offences.

You can see where this is going.

A tangle of corrupt officials, stupidly strict penal provisions and indifferent judges makes law reform near impossible (though you are heartened by the few states who have managed to legalize medical marijuana). One day you wonder if drugs should be legal; maybe you could even help make them legal. You are sick of hiding your powers, pretending to be mild-mannered when you could be awesome. Maybe a little bit of fear wouldn't be such a bad thing. Some of those powerful people should learn to fear something.

It's time to take the big step. It's time to be awesome. You come out openly, deciding that being a hero should be your full-time job. It turns out that crime doesn't only happen at night or on slow news days. Working a human job is just pointless, there's too much to get done. So now Superman protects the city—protects it from everyone. You set up a refuge for everyone who fears someone powerful. You tell the police that your friend will not be facing charges, they can't take him, they can't charge him, they can't incarcerate him. But that seems unfair, there are so many people unjustly imprisoned. So you bust out everyone on petty drug charges and give them a place in your refuge.

Next to go are the pimps. Sex work should be legal everywhere and men shouldn't be able to exploit women who would like to work safely, or force women into it who aren't willing. So, you take in all the sex workers and make clear that no pimps are welcome. If any pimps complain, you decide not to repeat the mistakes of so many superheroes, who are forever letting their nemeses get away and cause havoc another day. (Seriously, how many deaths are on Superman's head for letting Lex Luthor come back again and again?) So, some pimps get made an example of. If any complain, your combination of super hearing and laser eyesight make short work of them.

And so it goes on. You build a bigger and bigger city. There is no homelessness, no street violence, no domestic violence (abusive husbands fare quite badly under your reign). Drug use is legal and protected, as is sex work. Your city is starting to look more and more like a well-run Scandinavian country. As officials attempt to oppose you they are dealt with summarily. Of what importance is a mayor beholden to corporate interests? You appoint yourself mayor of the city, then president of the country. There can be no war, you can defeat any national army from the upper atmosphere with those awesome and too-often-forgotten laser eyes.

Are you a villain? In a sense, unquestionably. You violate every rule of official superherodom. You kill people. Relatively often. You have fun; not having to pretend you're a boring human, you get heaps of girls. You avoid that awkward bit where the girl you like is partly in love with both you and your alter-ego. She's just totally into all of you. Sure, you're a villain, but you're better than every superhero who never had the courage to do what you do: To genuinely use their powers to remake the world into the better place that humans wish they could but always fall short because they rely on consensus to do it.

And that's ultimately what it comes down to. There are lots of people who want the world to be a better place and a few who are powerful enough to make sure that never happens. You don't represent those in power, but you do represent a lot of others. And if that makes you a villain, well, the millions of dollars, beautiful women, and sense of accomplishment make it all worthwhile.

– B. C. Roberts, 2017

-:--:--:--:--:- *GS* -:--:--:--:--:-

TOP 13 ENTRIES

Top 13 Cinematic Sequels

7. INDIANA JONES AND THE TEMPLE OF DOOM (1984)

Sequel to: (except kind of prequel to) *Raiders of the Lost Ark* (1981)
Followed by: *Indiana Jones and the Last Crusade* (1989), *Indiana Jones and the Kingdom of the Crystal Skull* (2008)
Story by: George Lucas
Written by: Willard Huyck and Gloria Katz
Directed by: Steven Spielberg
Better than original? Not even close. It's still good but not in the same league. Even Spielberg doesn't like it.

> **MOLA RAMI:** Kali ma... Kali ma... Kali ma, shakthi deh!

In 1935, one year before the events of *Raiders*, Indiana Jones, the awesome Shorty Round and the unrelentingly awful Willie Scott find themselves in a caricatured India searching for magical stones which bring fortune and glory. Along the way we are treated to a famously unappetizing dinner party which includes dishes of eyeball soup and chilled monkey brains, a mine cart chase which was shot on a rollercoaster at Disneyland and the spectacle of a man's heart being mystically pulled from his chest to the immortal chant of what I was sure until this morning was 'kari-bah' but is, in fact, "Kali ma," an invocation to the much-maligned Indian deity after whom I named my cat. Though *Temple of Doom* is not an awful movie it suffers badly in comparison to the others in this trilogy (its status has now of course been saved by the unspeakable fourth entry). Even Spielberg says the only positive thing to come out of it was that he got in Kate Capshaw's pants.

– *B. C. Roberts, 2017*

Want to see the rest of the list? Check out *The Top 13 – From the Pages of Geek Speak Magazine*, out now.

-:--:--:--:--:- *GS* -:--:--:--:--:-

Top 13 Superheroes without Superpowers

9. KICK-ASS

Created by: Mark Millar and John Romita, Jr.
Year: 2008
Seen in: Kick-Ass is new to the world of underpowered superheroes and so far has appeared only in his seven issue comic book series and blockbuster 2010 motion picture, all entitled *Kick-Ass*.

Motto: Doesn't really have one, certainly not the sort of thing you yell out before going into battle. "Avengers Assemble" is a little naff for Kick-Ass. "Oh, fuck" is his most common refrain. His best line though, is: 'Why do people want to be Paris Hilton and nobody wants to be Spider-Man?'

Theme Song: "Kick Ass" by Mika. A power pop anthem which sounds like Elton John trying to do Guns 'n' Roses. Absolutely terrible.

Secret Identity: Dave Lizewski, average high school kid. Not the class jock, not the class geek.

Nickname: Dumbass and the like (mostly from Hit Girl).

Affiliation: Likes to hang with other superheroes. Almost joined a super group with Hit Girl and Big Daddy until their fourth member, superhero imposter Red Mist, sold them out to his father, crime boss Frank D'Amico.

Sidekick: Red Mist for about two days. That didn't end well. Particularly for Red Mist, who, in the comic, is killed by Kick-Ass. He survives to become a super-villain in the movie.

Romantic Entanglements: Dave is in love with Katie Deauxma. She becomes friends with him when she thinks he's gay, though he ultimately confesses that he isn't. In the comic she screams at him and texts him a picture of her blowing another guy. In the movie they get together and have fun sexy times.

Arch-Nemesis: Kick-Ass is way too small scale to have an arch nemesis. Frank D'Amico becomes one by default when he captures and tortures Kick-Ass and Big Daddy. When Frank kills Big Daddy, Kick-Ass helps Hit Girl take him down.

Powers and/or Proficiencies: Initially none whatsoever beyond optimism and naïveté. After his first unsuccessful foray into crime fighting Dave is left with a lot of metal in his skeleton and destroyed nerve endings, meaning he cannot feel much pain.

Source: Generally being lame; getting stabbed, and then hit by a car.

Weapon: Two bits of wood that probably have a cool name in Japanese that most of us don't know.

Origin Story: Dave is bored, and obsessed with comics. His dad works night shift, which gives him the freedom to run around costumed after dark. He is not fighting any great injustice or seeking to avenge anyone close to him; he's doing it just because he thinks it's a cool idea. And he loves the popularity once he's famous.

Why He's Super: Honestly, the Kick-Ass of the comics is kind of a loser. He is not the most proficient fighter (that title goes to Hit Girl by a mile) and he doesn't get the girl. In the movie Dave saves the day with a jet pack equipped with mounted machine guns and gets hot and steamy with Katie. In either case he does pretty well just to not die – that's kinda super.

– B. C. Roberts, 2010

Want to see the rest of the list? Check out *The Top 13 – From the Pages of Geek Speak Magazine*, out now.

-:--:--:--:--:- *GS* -:--:--:--:--:-

Top 13 Video Games

11. MASS EFFECT

Released: 2007
Platform: Xbox 360, later followed by PC and then even later by PS3 and Wii U (suckers!)
Created by: Bioware Enterprises
Published by: Electronic Arts
Subgenre: Action/RPG
Sequels and Spinoffs: *Mass Effect Galaxy* on iOS (2009), *Mass Effect 2* (2010), *Mass Effect 3* (2012), *Mass Effect Infiltrator* on iOS (2012)
Elsewhere: A series of novels and comics; an anime movie will be release in December this year, and a live-action movie is in development.
Players: 1, plus an online multiplayer component included in *Mass Effect 3*
Trivia: The ending to the trilogy sucked balls and prompted a social media campaign to have it changed.

Quote:

> "Why is it whenever someone says 'with all due
> respect,' they really mean 'kiss my ass'"?
> – Ashley Williams, *Mass Effect*

Mass Effect was a revelation in the early days of the Xbox 360. A game which combined sloppy shooter mechanics with an under-developed progression scheme and woefully complicated inventory management nonetheless boasted the closest thing to an interactive movie seen to that point. In the shoes of Commander Sheppard (your choice of male or female) players followed the story of humanity's early days on the galactic stage, trying to prove that we're not low-tech chumps by being willing to perform dangerous missions nobody else much cares about. Along the way you get the chance to Captain Kirk it up, wooing creatures from across the universe, success at which will get you short clips of soft porn. The inclusion of same-sex relationships was definitely a step forward for the typically macho games industry.

There are three central elements to *Mass Effect*'s greatness, despite its many technical shortcomings. First is a terrific story of slowly unfolding intrigue and betrayal culminating in a fight to save the Citadel, a shining beacon of inter-galactic bureaucracy. Second is a revolutionary dialogue mechanic. Rather than reading all the choices of dialogue response, Bioware offered up short summaries in the form of the general tone/point of the responses. This sped up the interactions and made them feel more spontaneous (you hadn't just read the words your character was now repeating).

The final element did not become clear until the first sequel but it is a surprising permanence of decisions. Characters created in the first game can be 'carried-over' to the sequels with all of their earlier decisions having permanent consequences on the later games. Kill a character in *Mass Effect 1*, you'll hear all about it from their friends in *Mass Effect 3*. The sheer programming that must go into putting that many options onto a couple of disks is mind boggling.

But this strength turned into an unforeseen problem. At the conclusion of the trilogy, players are given a choice between two endings of meaningless differences. After three games worth of accumulated choices, to narrow that vast range down to a couple of options makes all those earlier choices seem irrelevant. The hours and hours of thought players put into their interactions, into the type of hero they wanted to be, was greatly under-appreciated by the developers and the response they got from fans should not have surprised them so much.

HONORABLE ACTION/RPG MENTIONS: *Fallout* (*1, 2, 3, Las Vegas*), *The Legend of Zelda* (particularly *Ocarina of Time*), most later *Castlevania* games (particularly *Symphony of the Night*), *Diablo II*

12. PORTAL

Released: 2007
Platform: Xbox 360, PlayStation 3, PC
Created by: Valve Software
Developed by: Electronic Arts/Steam
Genre: First Person Shooter/Puzzler
Sequels and Spinoffs: *Portal 2* (2011)
Players: 1. 2-player co-op in *Portal 2*
Trivia: *Portal 2* originally wasn't going to have portals.

Quote:

> "We hope your brief detention in the relaxation vault
> has been a pleasant one."
> GLaDOS, *Portal*

I have to confess that I am just over halfway through the co-op of *Portal 2* with this magazine's illustrious Editor-in-Chief. I think she only asked me to write this to remind me.

The original *Portal* was released on the Orange Box, a spectacular collection of *Half Life 2*, its two episodic continuations, *Team Fortress 2* and *Portal*. Just a few hours long, *Portal* was a revelation and clearly the most innovative game of the year.

The premise of *Portal* is that you awake in a murderous testing chamber operated by the psychopathic GLaDOS (Genetic Lifeform and Disk Operating System) tasked with navigating your way through and ultimately out of the testing facility. Your only 'weapon', and the primary puzzle mechanic, is the Aperture Science Handheld Portal Device or portal gun. The portal gun allows you to shoot an entry and an exit portal through which objects and the player can pass. In the best puzzles you have to create entry portals in mid-air as you fall – the portals hold momentum so if you go in fast you come out just as fast and that can be up, down, sideways, any direction you can get a portal facing.

The genius of *Portal* is in the variety of puzzles and the lateral thinking required to solve them. And this was taken to the next level in the co-op of *Portal 2*. With two people and two portal guns the complexity of puzzles takes a major jump. Having one person jumping off a catapult to fly through a portal, come out in another direction and catch a box launched through their partner's portal is mind bending and awesome. It was a key part of *Portal 2* being awarded Game of the Year in 2011.

More than any other current game company, Valve makes innovative games, and *Portal* is the peak example.

HONORABLE STORY-ESQUE PUZZLE-Y MENTIONS:
King's Quest, Lemmings

– B. C. Roberts, 2012

Want to see the rest of the list? Check out *The Top 13 – From the Pages of Geek Speak Magazine*, out now.

-:--:--:--:--:- *GS* -:--:--:--:--:-

COLUMN: TAKING AIM

Why *Luke Cage*'s Fan Service is Out of Place in the MCU

This isn't a review of the *Luke Cage*, the latest Marvel/Netflix show. This wonderful magazine has already provided a comprehensive review, which hits all the important points but leaves out perhaps the strangest part of the whole series: the wedged in fan-service for long-time readers of the source comics. And I do mean *long-time*; some of this stuff is drawn from the first comics in the 70s, and was never revisited.

"Fan service" is a loose term that refers to pretty much anything introduced specifically to please fans, but is not explained to the casual reader or viewer. Since, presumably, the show/book/etc. is supposed to be already amusing, fan service normally refers to aspects which are not strongly connected to the main narrative. Traditionally, fan service (especially in manga) meant gratuitous nudity. And it's worth pointing out that there is precious little of that sort of fan service in the MCU generally. There is no shortage of beautiful women in the MCU but we never see them in bikinis slowly exiting the sea à la James Bond, the latest *Fast and Furious* and a hundred other action movies.

Instead, in the increasingly interconnected/complicated cross-over world of the Marvel Cinematic Universe, fan service has manifested in two main forms: (1) references to events in other parts of the MCU; and (2) references to the original source material.

The first of these is just boring. Everyone in every show from *Luke Cage* to *Daredevil* to *Agents of S.H.I.E.L.D.* refers to "The Incident" all the time (by which they mean that time aliens descended from the sky over New York and got beat up by a small number of supers). Claire Temple (Rosario Dawson) says she "knows a good lawyer" and we know she is referring to Matt Murdock (or maybe Foggy? Or maybe even Trinity, but probably Matt). References to magic hammers, super soldiers etc. abound. It's great, we get it, you guys made billions of dollars making comic book movies. We didn't think it was possible either! Let's all go get drunk and tell everyone how we convinced millions of people to watch a movie about Thor.

The second type of fan service – the comic book references – are somewhat different. They feel out of place for reasons I couldn't at the time of watching quite specify. But now that I have a terribly clever answer, let's consider three examples of comic book fan service in *Luke Cage* (which is not worse than on any other of the shows, it just happens to be the one I watched most recently) and then we'll work through why I think they don't belong.

1. Luke's original costume. Luke's costume of yellow shirt open to the waist, tight jeans and silver tiara is just basic-level comic book costume absurdity. It is no better or worse than Cyclops' blue jumpsuit or Wolverine's blue and yellow jumpsuit (I'm sensing a theme). When Luke escapes Seagate prison in the show, he pulls some clothes off a line which - amazingly - are exactly what 70s comics Luke used to wear. Not only is it surprising that such clothes can be found on a line in Georgia in the 21st century, it is even more surprising that Luke neglects to button up the shirt at all.

2. Misty' costume. The show's last look at Misty is her with a huge Afro and a top with cutout shoulders. This doesn't look anything like what she's worn for the entire show or like anything anybody has worn in a long time. Again, it's her iconic comic costume.

3. Misty losing her arm. Readers of the comics will know that Misty Knight has a bionic arm. When she gets shot in the show by Cottonmouth, Claire tells her: "You're lucky you didn't lose your arm." All the comic book readers must have been thinking, "oh my god this is when she's gonna lose her arm and get a cool new one made by Tony Stark." But it didn't happen and we are all the poorer for it.

4. Heroes for Hire. Luke Cage is perhaps most famous for running an agency with Misty Knight and Iron Fist called Heroes for Hire. And dear god did they harp on about this in the show. People repeatedly tell Luke, "we'd hire you for that sort of protection." Luke repeatedly

says, "I'm no hero," often in response to people suggesting he become a hero for hire.

So why do these somewhat innocuous examples annoy me? I think it's because the world of the Marvel movies in general, and the Marvel/Netflix shows in particular, is much more closely grounded in reality than the comic books are and whenever elements of the comics creep in they break with the realism and remind us of the completely crazy comic world.

Before everyone goes all, "the MCU is not even remotely grounded in reality," let's consider how much more fantastic the comics are. Like that time the Hulk got shot into space, landed on a weird planet, became a hero to the slaves, led them in a revolt against the king, fought and killed the king, became the new king, fell in love, had a baby and then the whole planet exploded and he went back the Earth.

Or the time Aunt May got shot and Peter did a deal with the devil to bring her back to life and had to sacrifice his marriage with Mary Jane to do so and consequently he went back in time but the timelines still matched up later on with the other comics once everyone got bored of Spider-Man being in the 60s.

And let's not even talk about Secret Invasion.

The MCU doesn't have to be realistic but it does have a consistency to its reality which diverges less from daily life than the comics do. And the costumes are particularly a part of that. The gritty costumes of the Luke Cage show have nothing in common with their garish comic counterparts.

So maybe Marvel could stick with the jeans, hoodies and generally normal clothes without always trying to appease the hardcore fans who must by now be vastly outnumbered by the casuals.

– B. C. Roberts, 2016

-:--:--:--:--:- *GS* -:--:--:--:--:-

What the Hell is Going On with *Civil War II* Continuity?

I am not a die-hard comic reader/lover/fanboy/whatever. I started reading comics when *Civil War I* was covered in the mainstream press (Peter Parker, why did you reveal your secret identity, why?) and I stopped when life got too busy to justify buying ten comics a week just to flick through them listlessly.

But right now I am living overseas, stay-at-home-parenting my two superhero-loving sons, and wading into *Civil War II* seemed like a harmless way to while away the tropical nights.

And mostly it is. But as I spend another night drinking cheap local beer and reading about the exploits of the newly reincarnated-as-a-Hydra-agent Steve Rogers, the stridently-certain-with-the-power-to-destroy-planets Captain Marvel (who is a girl; girls can destroy planets too), and the I'm-pretending-I'm-conflicted-but-I'm-really-pretty-fucking-certain-I'm-right Iron Man, I find I lose track of where this sentence is going. Nope, got it. I'm discovering that I don't know why I stopped watching Netflix to read these in the first place.

Not because they're not good. They're not, obviously. But the bar for comics is set pretty low. They're thankfully not allowed to be shamelessly exploitative anymore (although someone forgot to tell the makers of the new *Killing Joke* movie) but they remain determinedly silly. As I realized when I tried to explain to my son today that Steve Rogers/Captain America had been resurrected/given his super powers back by a newly sentient tesseract-thingy except the little girl tesseract-thing had been brainwashed by Red Skull and so she brought Captain America back as a secret Hydra Agent.

Exactly.

And it's not about the ludicrously costly barrier to entry. Many have already complained about needing to spend $40 a week to know what is going on in the ten or more different books that are all tied in to this 'main event.' The ridiculous cost is indeed a barrier but I have a different gripe with the hundred or so comics covering the same event from different angles.

Enough prelude. Now to the not very important stuff.

Civil War II involves a new fight between superheroes split over the – oh, God, I can't even bear to recount it. Every single Marvel comic of the last four months has begun with a summary of the existence of a new Inhuman called Ulysses who can see the future, and the existential dilemma of whether superheroes should act on such foreknowledge, or if doing so amounted to punishing people before they did anything wrong (*Minority Report*, anyone?) making it kind of profiling. Dammit. I accidentally recounted it anyway.

Right. So they split over whether to use this kid's powers and Iron Man says 'No way, that's really bad, I'm a futurist but the future isn't written' and Captain Marvel says 'I may just be a small town intergalactic space avenger slash loveable aunt but I'm still tough, and sexy' (thanks, Dixie Normous) 'and I am going to stop bad things before they happen.' Then Ulysses has a vision that Thanos is coming to Earth to steal some irrelevant but incredibly powerful/dangerous maguffin and Captain Marvel gets some good guys together to go stop him but clearly she doesn't get enough because (Spoiler Alert, but you don't really care) James 'Rhodey' Rhodes (that's right, his nickname is just his normal name with a 'y' instead of an 's' on the end) gets killed. Rhodey is both Iron Man's best friend and Captain Marvel's secret lover. But Iron Man takes precedence in the grief stakes because bromance beats romance every day of the superhero week (which, incidentally, has an unspoken additional eighth day for polishing your outfit, courtesy of Doctor Strange).

So here is where I end the torturous intro and get to the point. Over the months of *Civil War II* lead ups and tie-ins, James Rhodes has died, and come back to life only to die again, at least three times. Because apparently the most powerful entertainment corporation in the world, the corporation that can make a sequel about a lost fish and still make you love it, cannot manage to organize some continuity between ten fucking comic books. There are six issues of *Invincible Iron Man* dealing with the lead up to *Civil War II* (starting as far back as February), except that *Civil War II* #1 (July, 2016), when Rhodey gets killed, was published in the middle of those issues' being released.

Similarly, there are separate comics centering on Ulysses himself, which all deal with the time between *Civil War II* #1 and #2 (I apologize for the naming conventions, they're obviously not mine) but are published between 1&2 then between 2&3 and then 3&4. So they deal with stuff that we know will already happen a certain way. Making it somewhat strange to go back to the having doubts in the garden of Gethsemane bit when we know the decision that is going to be made.

The same thing happens with She-Hulk, who gets injured in the same fight with Thanos but then appears in other, later, comics. And also when Bruce Banner gets shot through the head by Hawkeye even though he got cured by Amadeus Cho (if you understand that sentence, congratulations, you're a terrific geek). And further when Hawkeye kills Bruce Banner, goes to trial and has his verdict released – two weeks later he is still in custody helping Captain Marvel with her problems in *Captain Marvel #8*.

So, bearing in mind that I'm an unusually time-rich customer, and it is entirely possible that Marvel isn't actually expecting anyone to purchase – at US$4 each – every single *Civil War II* tie-in, it still seems kind of lazy that their big 2016 let's-cash-in-on-*Captain America: Civil War* event is... kind of lazy.

I will, of course, keep reading the series to the bitter end – only a few weeks away now – because it remains an excellent way to pass drunken tropical nights. Though the awesomeness of Rajinikanth movies may ultimately squeeze the ridiculousness of Marvel comics out of my life. And if it does, I might actually just forget to find out how the superheroes ultimately get reconciled and the whole thing amounts to absolutely no long-term effect because, hey, it was all secret Skrulls who were responsible, anyway.

Seriously Marvel, if you're reading, I swear to god if you explain away *Captain America: Civil War* so glibly, I will stop watching *Daredevil, Jessica Jones, Agents of S.H.I.E.L.D.* and probably even *Luke Cage*. And I'd threaten *Agent Carter* but we both know I couldn't stay away and then you cancelled her anyway. And I won't see your new movie on the opening day. And at some point I will have a proper think about how much of your media I'm consuming and whether or not that's a healthy thing.

And THEN you'll be in trouble.

– B. C. Roberts, 2016

Why *Ghost in the Shell* is the Best (Non-Miyazaki) Anime, by Far

BATOU: And what are you going to talk about? You don't even remember your own name. You stupid dickhead.

There is often something deeply unsatisfying about anime as a Western viewer. For every masterpiece like *Akira* or pretty much any Studio Ghibli production there are hundreds of thrillingly bland series like *Bubblegum Crisis*.

Whether or not it was the first anime I watched I no longer remember, but for me anime is viewed through the lens of *Neon Genesis Evangelion* – the hugely popular and awfully disappointing series from the 1990's. *Neon Genesis* follows Shinji, a boy on the verge of adolescence who, along with Asuka (who is German, obviously) and Rei, pilots hugely powerful mechs called Evas. Earth is under attack from aliens and these kids must use this ridiculous power to stop them.

Perfect setup for amazing large scale, Power Rangers-style battles that decimate cities right? Hmm, sadly not so much.

Because, like most anime, *Neon Genesis* has an undercurrent of just plain fucking crazy. It's not enough to have robots fighting aliens apparently. Instead it is clearly necessary to have an odd semi-Biblical element whereby the progenitor-thing of the Evas is a creature called Lilith (Eve and Lilith, I'm sure you can draw the links) and to have the aliens called Angels (with the connotation that God is waging an assault on the world).

None of it makes any sense whatsoever and for the longest time I thought that I was missing something in the translation – which is extremely common when adult anime like *Dragonball* and *One Piece* are repurposed for Western children. Did you know that most of *One Piece* is really filthy and most characters voice sentiments to Nami similar to what most 15-year-olds think of her (if you believe the pornographic fan fiction and fan art)? Only the other day did I discover that, apparently frustrated by the batshit insanity of *Neon Genesis*, the producers cut the budget, and the main reason the ending makes even less sense than the rest of the show is because they had no money to use more than existing backdrops with dialogue over the top.

So this is the background necessary to understand when I talk about the 1995 anime version of *Ghost in the Shell* (the live action version of which, controversially starring Scarlett Johansson, is released this Friday). Because, miraculously, *Ghost in the Shell* doesn't suck at all. And the mandatory 'important themes' even make sense in the context of the rest of the movie. *Ghost* follows Major Motoko Kusanagi of Section 9, a division of the Hong Kong government (the manga and other anime are set in Japan but weirdly the movie is set in Hong Kong). Kusanagi has a completely cybernetic body but it houses her real human brain and her 'ghost', which is really kind of shorthand for a soul. Kusanagi is chasing the Puppetmaster, a person who has been hacking the ghosts of other people for unknown reasons.

The action and everything else in this movie is fabulous, as directed by the now-legendary Mamoru Oshii. But the best part is the whole question about whether machines can have souls. The difference between Kusanagi with her robot body and the puppet master, who is a self-aware AI inside a similar robot body, is intriguing. And the overall question of what does it mean to be human when cybernetic enhancement is the norm and you can hack human brains is so much more sensible than what does it mean to be an adolescent piloting a giant robot as angels attack the earth, etc.

Ghost in the Shell has a 96% Fresh rating on Rotten Tomatoes, so most of you already know that the movie is amazing. And let's be honest, most of you have probably noticed that most anime gets pretty crazy at some point. But really the thing that sets *Ghost in the Shell* apart is that it manages to put together a healthy amount of action (not as much as *Akira*, obviously), some random nudity (nowhere near as much as *Ninja Scroll*) and a sensible, coherent and interesting plot (unlike pretty much all of them).

– B. C. Roberts, 2017

-:--:--:--:--:- *GS* -:--:--:--:--:-

For the Love of *Dellamorte Dellamore*

Based on the novel by Tiziano Sclavi and directed by Michele Soavi, the 1994 cult classic *Dellamorte Dellamore* – AKA *Cemetery Man* – is that old story of boy meets girl, boy falls in love with girl, girl dies, girl comes back as a zombie, boy kills girl, girl comes back as a real zombie, boy realizes last time she wasn't a zombie, boy kills girl again.

Francesco Dellamorte (Rupert Everett) is the watchman of the Buffalora cemetery. In his cemetery (and perhaps elsewhere) seven days after their death corpses rise from the grave. Francesco, simply because it's his job he supposes, kills the 'returners' and prevents them from over-running the small town.

It is quite hard to explain exactly what it is about this movie that I love. At a superficial level it has lots of zombies, heaps of violence and plenty of sex. But it's also fused with this ridiculous Italian absurdity that I find addictive.

There are three particularly odd aspects that make the movie for me:

1. The way that unsubstantiated rumors are treated as absolutely true.
2. Dellamorte's assistant Gnaghi, whose only word is Gna.
3. The film's inexplicable ending.

Rumors

Some thugs in the town have spread the rumor that Francesco is impotent. When Anna Falchi's character (listed in the title only as She) is killed by her zombie husband, the doctor's examination reveals that she was having sex when she died. The police chief immediately excludes Francesco from suspicion, despite the death occurring in the small cemetery with nobody else around.

Later in the movie when Francesco starts to unhinge and shoots the thugs who started the rumor, the police chief finds Francesco with a gun and says: 'Great, you've got a gun to defend yourself.' Apparently his rumored impotence extends to an inability to kill.

Gnaghi

Gnaghi (François Hadji-Lazaro) is a strange-looking, mentally handicapped man. One day he meets the Mayor's daughter Valentina (Fabiana Formica) and falls in love with her. She is decapitated in a motorcycle accident the next day and when she rises from her grave, Gnaghi decides to keep her head in a hollowed out TV. The maintain a 'relationship' for months with Valentina only occasionally trying to bite him. Gnaghi is devastated when Francesco ultimately re-kills her when she begins to smell.

The Ending

At the end of the movie Francesco and Gnaghi finally decide it is time to leave Buffalora and discover the rest of the world. As they reach the city-limits the road gives out and there is nothing but a deep canyon. Francesco realizes that there is no 'rest of the world', there is only Buffalora and working in the cemetery. There is no explanation for why Buffalora is the only place in the world, we only know that there is no escape for our heroes.

This movie made almost no money and received poor critical reviews. Nonetheless, like so many other strangely compelling genre movies, it is much better and way more rewarding than the figures suggest.

– B. C. Roberts, 2017

-:--:--:--:--:- *GS* -:--:--:--:--:-

ESSAYS

Iron Fist, Season 1: A Conversation, by Rachel Hyland and B. C. Roberts

Iron Fist. Season 1 of this latest installment of the Marvel Netflix franchise was released in its entirety on March 17, 2017 and now, over a month later, *Geek Speak*'s Rachel Hyland and B. C. Roberts have both finally made their respective ways through this most disappointing of offerings. Here, a conversation spanning the unprecedented *weeks* it took them to get through the show, with obscenity-laden commentary on same...

-- SPOILERS FOR ALL EPISODES OF *IRON FIST* --

Tuesday, March 21

B. C. ROBERTS:

So, *Iron Fist*?

RACHEL HYLAND

Am three episodes in and cannot recall the last time I groaned so much during a show, and that includes *The Big Bang Theory*. Danny is just so... dumb. And it kind of makes sense, he's a 10-year-old in a kung fu master's body, but the acting is so inscrutable and the writing so weak that you have to work so hard to make allowances that it's annoying – and you know me, I'm usually happy to fill in plot holes.

Maybe if *Arrow* didn't exist, I wouldn't be so disappointed.

BCR:

I'm six episodes in. I completely agree that the acting and writing are so weak that it's hard to figure out what they're going for most of the time. Sometimes Danny is super serious and then he's like an excited child and then he's weirdly trusting and then he's all determined and certain. And it just doesn't come together at all.

It's the stupidest Marvel thing in a long, long time.

Friday, March 24

RH:

RE: Episode 6, "Immortal Emerges from Cave"

I had high hopes for this *Mortal Kombat*-style tournament. And then the stupid spider girl...

BCR:

Yeah that was ridiculous.
It keeps getting worse. Hard to believe but it's a train wreck. I can't understand quite how they managed to fuck it up so comprehensively.

Monday, March 27

BCR:

My God. 13 episodes is far too many. This show just keeps on being awful and keeps on going and going and going.

Wednesday, March 29, 2017

BCR:

I finished *Iron Fist* last night. I'm dying to hear what you think of the whole thing.

RH:

Yes, doubtless we will have much to discuss. It might be a while...

Saturday, April 1

RE: Episode 7, "Felling Tree with Roots"

RH:

"About last night... I enjoyed it." Ugh.

BCR:

At least he said he enjoyed it. I was so worried he was going to go all "I'm a celibate monk, I've made a terrible mistake."

RH:

Poor Colleen. First he spends hours lecturing this KUNG FU TEACHER on how to kung fu, and then he somehow gets her to sleep with him.

RE: Episode 9, "The Mistress of All Agonies"

RH:

Danny's not very smart, is he? He brought Gao all the way back from China to... NOT torture her for information? And none of these conversations could have been had on the plane home?

BCR:

I have genuinely no idea why he kidnapped Gao or even how he did it. What happened to her blow Danny across the room hand of power thing?

RH:

Yes! So ludicrous. They clearly forgot about that. Meanwhile, Gao is namechecking all of Claire's super-powered buds... it is ballsy of them to point out the blatant happenstance. And at least Claire doesn't know Jessica Jones! (Although, she IS Claire's boyfriend's ex...)

At some point, if you're Claire, you just have to think maybe it's you.

BCR:

I think my problems with *Iron Fist* come down to two main things: first is that Finn Jones is just an awful actor. The writing is clearly trying to go for some brooding intensity (which was a poor choice) but he just cannot pull it off in the slightest; second is *Arrow*. This whole thing has been DONE BEFORE.

It's like the only thing that DC has already nailed

Also, I love Rosario Dawson but turning Claire into a fighter just to keep her relevant is stupid. She's a way shittier character now than she was in the first season of *Daredevil*.

RE: Episode 10, "Black Tiger Steals Heart"

RH:

Is that Danny on the cover of *Forbes* magazine?!? Calling him an "entrepreneur"?

BCR:

Oh my god. I missed that.

RH:

Insane. He's been back for a minute and a half. When did he have time for a cover shoot?

BCR:

There's always time for a cover shoot.

RH:

Can we talk about Bakuto (Ramon Rodriguez) for a second? Bakuto is by far the best thing to happen to this show in its entire run, except for maybe when poor dead Kyle (Alex Wyse) dared to like vanilla ice cream. And by best I mean most surprising, I didn't want Kyle to die horribly, you understand. But having Harold beat him to death – wow. I did not expect that at all. And likewise, Bakuto. He is The Hand! Colleen is The Hand! But the good kind of Hand, except not really, still all gangster control-the-world-y, but just really smooth about it. And Colleen has basically been recruiting kids into the Foot Clan this whole time.

BCR:

But then she turned on her sensei in a second when Danny needed her to, because of sex, I guess? Bakuto really needs to get himself a Bebop and Rocksteady.

And we really should just have watched the *Teenage Mutant Ninja Turtles* instead of this show.

RH:

Truth!

Sunday, April 9, 2017

RE: Episode 11, "Lead Horse Back to Stable"

RH:

Danny just spent a whole episode NOT being the Iron Fist. This show should have been entitled *Mostly Normal Fist*.

BCR:

Hahahahaha. It is just relentlessly bad. The whitewashing isn't even in the top ten of its failings

Sunday, April 16, 2017

RE: Episode 13, "Dragon Plays with Fire"

RH:

So, did Harold think that Joy would believe Danny somehow worked with the Hand to sell the drugs through Rand (heh, Rand... The Hand...) BEFORE HE CAME BACK TO NEW YORK? While he was in an ancient, mythical monastery? And had no access to the company, or anything?

BCR:

No fucking idea what Harold was thinking. Worst deflection of blame ever.

RH:

And OF COURSE Harold had Danny's parents killed.

BCR:

Of course.

RH:

Hey, *Iron Fist*! Even *Revenge of the Sith* thinks your reveal is obvious and super lame.

RH:

Whew. Almost done now. It's just Davos and Joy talking and... um... WHAT THE HELL, DAVOS?!?

BCR:

Fucking Davos. Makes no sense whatsoever. So, can I assume that you've seen it now and I can start talking about everyone to the end?

RH:

Yep. Spoilers no more!

BCR:

Hooray... First, why were they so surprised that Kunlun had gone? Surely the way had to close eventually?

RH:

Or did the Hand, who are – after all – the sworn enemies of Kunlun, cause it to close after they were able to invade due to the lack of a reliable Iron Fist? There are all those dead fighters, after all... I don't think Davos could have expected it to be closed so soon; or perhaps he did, and blames Danny for exiling him from his home which is why he suddenly wants to kill him, and not for the tedious unrequited love reason that they seem to be going for.

BCR:

I agree that's what the implication was, but it seemed like "the way" was open for a terribly long time. Enough time for Danny to leave, run down a mountain, fight in illegal fight clubs, get a fake passport, get to New York and then do everything in the show. If the way to Kunlun only open every 15 years, it seems like it's been open for at least a year?

Of course I should have spelled that K'un-Lun, because Marvel.

RH:

The timeline on the show is definitely messed up. But I don't think Danny has been away from Kunlun – OF COURSE it is K'un-Lun, geez Marvel, way to exoticize – for all that long.

The final episode was, at least, the... less bad among them all. (Except for the coda. The coda can bite me.)

BCR:

Really? I thought the shift of good guys and bad guys was ridiculously unbelievable. Ward is now a good guy and Joy and Davos become bad guys. How is that even remotely likely? Joy has been consistently smarter than starting up some death plot against the fucking Iron Fist. Why do people always think that killing a superhero will be a walk in the park?

RH:

I have more faith in Joy. I think she is drawing out Davos to hear his nefarious plan and then will run straight to Danny to warn him. I could see her plotting Ward's death – he's betrayed her every day for over a decade, and then got her shot – but she is very fond of Danny and isn't nearly as ruthless as Davos seems to think. Unless the second death of her dad flipped that switch. (Which can happen in comic land, certainly.)

Ward being the good guy now makes more sense – he was always presented to us in a fairly sympathetic light, not in an anti-hero way or in a Fisk-esque fascinating villain way, but as a victim.

BCR:

I hope you're right. On the upside, we are not going to have to see them for, what, around 3 years?

RH:

Hopefully. The burning question in all of this, of course: DID ANYONE EVER FIND KYLE'S BODY?

BCR:

A better question: will you watch Season 2 of this awfulness?

RH:

Oh, you know. Probably. But it's, well, *Iron Fist*, so I won't exactly be in a fever of anticipation.

BCR:

Obviously.

RH:

You?

BCR:

Ask me again after *The Defenders*.

***Iron Fist* is available on Netflix.**

– Rachel Hyland and B. C. Roberts, 2017

-:--:--:--:--:- *GS* -:--:--:--:--:-

Sense8, Season 2: A Conversation, by Rachel Hyland and B. C. Roberts

Sense8. Brainchild of *Babylon 5*'s Michael J. Straczynski and *The Matrix*'s Wachawskis, it is the tale of eight individuals from around the world linked by a psychic connection, who can possess each other's bodies and who are hunted by a shadowy government organization out to capture and control them.

Here, a transcript of a conversation between *Geek Speak*'s B. C. Roberts and Rachel Hyland about the ten episodes of Season 2, released on May 5, 2017, along with the Christmas episode that launched on December 23, 2016.

-- SPOILERS FOR ALL EPISODES OF *SENSE8* --

B. C. ROBERTS:

The Christmas episode was weak, though everything with Kala (Tina Desai) in it is wonderful. And the orgy was a bit much. But the season gets better from there. And at least Will (Brian J. Smith) wasn't a smack head for the entire season, which I was worried about.

RACHEL HYLAND:

The Christmas episode was indeed lackluster, so much so that I can barely remember it. But yes, Kala is excellent; Kala and Wolfgang (Max Riemelt) are my favorite relationship, for sure.

Will is... problematic. His whole story arc, alongside Riley (Tuppence Middleton), gets pretty tangled.

BCR:

Riley is so bland. I don't even entirely understand what they are going for with her character. She's a super-chill DJ who fights really hard to help Will, but can't really muster up enough enthusiasm to look like she actually cares?

She mostly (so far at least) is intent on risking everything to have romantic sexy times.

Which I generally support, but does seem kind of reckless.

RH:

But stuff with Riley does improve, don't you think? Especially after she goes to Chicago. But she really doesn't bring much to the cluster, does she? Like, Nomi (Jamie Clayton) is a crazy good hacker, Sun (Doona Bae) and Wolfgang have the combat covered, Will's the lead investigator, Kala is the medic, Lito (Miguel Ángel Silvestre) emotes and persuades, Capheus (Toby Onwumere) can drive a bus. But Riley's just... from Iceland.

(Not that I would add much to a cluster either. At least Riley offers underworld drug contacts.)

BCR:

I wonder when they were designing the eight of them if they thought hard about the mix of skills you might want in a cluster. A cop, a hacker and a fighter are essential. I guess a driver is handy and Wolfgang is a general hard ass. I even quite like having Lito as the actor. I'm surprised they didn't go for a doctor, it seems like Kala is an unusually skilled lab scientist.

But then, what else would you have but a DJ to get the party started? How could they shoot all those ecstatic parties/orgies without someone controlling the tunes?

RH:

Those Wachowskis do love a rave scene.

I suppose if a cluster birth is supposed connect eight people with complementary temperaments and skills in order to create a sum bigger than their parts (and who all happen to be born on the same day), then a DJ/helpmeet is a useful inclusion.

The other interesting thing is how they all have deep-seated issues brought about by at least one parent – even Kala, who is the only one with a good relationship with both, undergoes an arranged marriage because of them.

BCR:

True. Do you think that's deliberate or just lazy? Like they accidentally created parent issues with each of the characters so they'd be suitably tortured?

RH:

Parental issues are kind of a go-to, aren't they? But there's a reason very few superheroes, for example, come from a happy home life rejoicing in a complete set of parents. It's the conflict that fuels the story.

Sun's brother killing their dad last season kicked off her whole arc, really. And second only to Kala/Wolfgang for me in this show is all things Sun.

BCR:

Sun really is wonderful. I love how they turned the prison thing around to it being really supportive of her. And the way she was quite hopeful despite being imprisoned.

But I also really like Nomi and Martha *[Amanita, played by Freema Agyeman – Ed.]* Who knew the Wachowskis were the answer to the question: "How do I see a Doctor's companion naked?"? Apart from the character being great, it's genuinely remarkable they've chosen a trans actor to play a trans character and given her a proper role that manages to be open about her gender without wallowing in it voyeuristically. If that makes any sense at all?

RH:

Yes, and how good is Freema Agyeman's American accent? Nothing like that stentorian, Dave-Chapelle-White-Guy-Voice you often hear from English actors, cf. Benedict Cumberbatch in *Doctor Strange*.

Jamie Clayton is terrific—not always the greatest actress but is always solid on the trans material, which must have been pretty important to Lana and Lilly.

Where do you stand on new Capheus?

BCR:

He's too pretty. He's also too fit and looks generally too competent.

RH:

I miss Capheus v.1's exuberance. But new Capheus comes into his own.

BCR:

I do think the two actors are different enough to find it quite jarring. I wonder what Aml Ameen said to Lana to get kicked out like that?

RH:

Is that what happened? Wow.

BCR:

That's the rumor that everybody repeatedly says they won't comment on.

RH:

Yeah, just checked. "Creative differences." Huh. Maybe it turned out he prefers Steven Seagal.

BCR:

Hahahahahaha. What did you think of the "faces change" conversation between Capheus and his friend? Seemed weirdly meta.

RH:

Oh, the "faces change" made me smile. It was almost *Supernatural* in its fourth wall, if not breaking, certainly leaning against.

BCR:

I have to say, though, I'm very disappointed in the finale. They did a *True Blood*. Nothing happens for the whole season and then the only time anything of importance actually happens is in the last ten minutes of the season and now I desperately want to watch the next season even though I know nothing of importance will actually happen in that season for almost all of it until, again, the last ten minutes. Ugh.

RH:

It does seem to be the new normal, narrative-wise. *The Walking Dead* does it too. Also *Game of Thrones*, really.

We are definitely looking at this from different perspectives, however, since I am probably more invested in the relationships than the plot and so feel like much of importance actually *has* happened.

BCR:

Sure. Kala and Wolfgang's relationship has moved forward. But otherwise? Nomi and Martha are getting married (but who cares?), Lito is in Hollywood now but is basically the same, Sun failed to kill her brother, Will and Riley are both crap. And Capheus is a popular hero.

There were some ridiculously cool scenes towards the end though. The restaurant shoot-out was spectacular.

RH:

Agreed. Wolfgang is a badass anyway, but having everyone – even Kala – involved there made it so much cooler. Their cluster versus demon lady Lila's cluster was so well-shot.

But let's not forget Sun and the detective (Sukku Son). LOVED that!

BCR:

Yeah, the detective was great. Their whole dynamic was cool.

RH:

And the end has us with all our sensates in the same place, with the bad guy. And he is a pretty good bad guy, that Whispers (Terrence Mann), super-creepy. It's just a shame they had to demystify that whole organization with the backroom corporate politics stuff. Here we thought he was the head honcho of... is it the BPO? That's right, the Biological Protection Organization. Because that's not a sinister-sounding name or anything.

BCR:

Yeah. And they drive around with it just emblazoned on their vans, no worries, nothing to see.

RH:

They're not that great at covert, it is true. And then Jonas (Naveen Andrews). What the hell was all that with Jonas?

BCR:

Yeah, I don't know. Is he a double agent, now? A triple agent?

RH:

The weirdest thing about the whole show, I think, is how it swings back and forth between kind of petty concerns – Lito's acting career, Nomi's bridesmaid's dress, Kala's marriage, etc. – and then there's all this the big world-shaking stuff threatening the cluster at the same time.

BCR:

Yeah, crazy how long it took someone to suggest to Lito he just leave Mexico and make a film in Hollywood. I thought he was going to make the connection when he saw his films had a cult following in the US, and when Bug (Michael X. Sommers) was mouthing along with his dialogue. Why did it take him so long?

RH:

Oh. Reasons. And you know what, I think calling Will and Riley "crap" is a bit harsh. For one thing, it's interesting, the way that their love story changes once they take the blockers, so they can't hear each other's thoughts – it's like they're in a long-distance relationship but are in the same room.

Aside from that, sure, they are pretty tiresome, but most of that is because they're forced to deal with the whole BPO situation while everyone else is out and about living their lives. Getting help from the cluster just to get acting jobs and beat up anyone attacking them. (And they all get attacked a lot.)

BCR:

Yeah, true. Will has to take heroin to hide from Whispers and keep the cluster safe, and then we cut to Capheus just driving his bus around and dating that beautiful journalist.

RH:

Yeah, and now Capheus is in politics, while Will, Nomi and Sun are infamous criminals. Everyone's getting really important.

BCR:

Don't forget Wolfgang, poised to take over the Berlin criminal underworld. And Kala, finding out that her rich husband's pharmaceutical company is selling expired AIDS drugs. She's going to blow the whistle on that for sure.

RH:

Especially because they're probably selling the drugs to Capheus's mother! Also, Lito was already famous, and Riley was apparently so well-loved as a DJ that she can get away with spinning *one track* at a club and still have people crazy about her. The Australian guy from *Speed Racer* dyeing his hair to be like her, even.

BCR:

Yeah, I didn't really understand what that was all about. Good seeing other sensates out there, though. It was like in *Matrix Reloaded*, when we meet the other humans who are fighting against the machines.

Interesting to see where they go with it all. So, who's your favorite character?

RH:

Sun. You?

BCR:

Kala.

RH:

Least favorite?

BCR:

Riley. You?

RH:

Same. You going to watch Season 3?

BCR:

Absolutely. You are, of course.

RH:

Of course! If only to find out if Bug ever gets to meet Lito. He'll faint.

***Sense8* is available on Netflix.**

– Rachel Hyland and B. C. Roberts, 2017

-:--:--:--:--:- *GS* -:--:--:--:--:-

Sex and Death and Emptiness – Why Season 5 of *True Blood* Left Me Cold

It turns out it *is* possible to get over beautiful naked vampires.

From its opening with a near-dead Tara, shot by were-trash Debbie, to its close with Bill drinking Lilith's blood and turning into some kind of blood monster/god, Season 5 of *True Blood* was a roller coaster of action and intrigue.

Of course, anybody who actually watched the latest season of *True Blood* would know what a shameful fucking lie that is.

The people involved in the creation of *True Blood* have a unique skill, and one that I haven't come across in any of the too-many shows I've watched over the years. Despite filling each instalment with as much sex, violence and drama as possible, at the end of each episode it still feels like nothing really happened. It's a skill they perfected in the last season – my god, Marnie (Fiona Shaw) was so boring, and having her killed by the ghost of Granny Stackhouse (Lois Smith) was so lame – and carried through into this one, especially when it came down to the last third of the season.

The season started incredibly strongly with "Turn! Turn! Turn!", an opening episode that delivered on every level and made promises we knew the following eleven episodes weren't going to be able to keep. At the end of Season 4, Tara (Rutina Wesley) had taken a bullet for Sookie (Anna Paquin), and is now near death. Vampire Pam (Kristin Bauer van Straten), estranged from her maker, is convinced to turn Tara into a vampire to save her life, in exchange for Sookie using her "super snatch" (my favorite line of the show so far) to reconcile Pam with Sookie's erstwhile lover, the thousand year-old vampire Eric (Alexander Skarsgård).

At the same time another of Sookie's erstwhile lovers, vampire Bill (Stephen Moyer), has just teamed with Eric to kill Chancellor Nan Flanagan (Jessica Tuck). Flanagan, the preachy public face of the American Vampire League, was supposed to have them killed for saving all vampires from Marnie (they weren't supposed to kill humans, even witches, or something or other) but Eric was, well, quicker off the mark. The two uncomfortable allies – or some other cliché for two people who need to work together despite not really liking each other – are trying to clean up the mess before the cavalry arrives to carry out their death sentences, all the more assured with the Chancellor's killing; they are, of course, too late and are captured as they try to flee. This, incidentally, gets in the way of them helping Sookie in her fight with Debbie (Brit Morgan)—who wanted to kill her because, well, honestly, I can't even remember and it doesn't really matter. (Sookie naturally gets away with Debbie's murder consequence free.

Awesomeness continues when Bill and Eric escape only to discover that Eric's "sister" Nora (Lucy Griffiths), another Chancellor of the Authority, had already arranged to save them. She has arranged their passage out of town with new identities, but not before they are forced to lay low for the daylight and give Eric and Nora the chance to engage in a little brother-sister reunion. "We fight like siblings, but we fuck like champions" is one of Eric's better lines, and a welcome return to him being a badass after being so boring with his memory gone throughout Season 4.

By far the highlight of the episode, though, is Sookie back to her ambivalent best. Dressed in a cute apron and pink rubber gloves she looks the picture of domestic bliss while scrubbing Debbie's brains out of the grouting. The juxtaposition of Sookie as traditional Southern girl and super-hot vampire bait has always been one of the series' strengths.

But from there it all goes rapidly downhill. The high points of each episode are always undermined by slow pacing and a whole lot of padding. Bill and Eric's use of the revelation that Russell Edgington[1] (Denis O'Hare) is alive as a bargaining chip to save their lives: awesome. But then dragged out for far too long, as it takes them multiple episodes to find him: boring. Tara pole-dancing at Fangtasia: hot. But countered by Salome's (Valentina Servi) casual and constant Kate Middleton-esque scrawny nakedness: not. Russell proclaiming himself the ultimate badass and telling Salome – Salome from *The Bible*! – to fuck off: spectacular. But then being killed before the opening credits of episode 12: just so disappointing.

I think the big development that is least well explained from this recent season is Bill's move to the dark side. I've heard from people who have read the books on which the show is based that Sookie and Eric eventually end up together even after he regains his memory, but it was never clear that the show was going to go in the same direction. Even halfway through this season it looked like they were setting Bill up as Sookie's one true love, and then suddenly, the guy who had always avoided killing humans is signing up to the sanguinista cause and treating people like food. And the vague explanations given – that they are all in a nest, that Bill doesn't feel guilty for being a vampire any more – don't give due weight to the transformation we are being expected to believe of the series' one-time hero. It all seemed largely implausible to me. Not least because all the other batshit insane things Bill and Eric do are normally explained by their mostly implausible devotion to Sookie, but this time she isn't even around, and instead is stuck in Bon Temps pouting earnestly over having killed Debbie.

Normally, it is the sub-plots that provide the most interest in *True Blood*. Last season, the plot given to Sookie's bar-owning, shape-shifting boss Sam Merlotte (Sam Trammell) was the clear winner. His relationships with his brother Tommy (Marshall Allman) and his fellow shifter Luna (Janina Gavankar) were nuanced and complicated. Tommy was the tortured soul whose past got in the way of him connecting with his brother, much as he might want to. And Luna was a revelation as a fiercely protective mother burdened with a violent ex-partner who just also happened to be the local werewolf pack leader. This season, Sam and Luna were great again, though they were given much less to work with.

And really the only touching moment of the whole season fell to the least important series regular, Hoyt Fortenberry (Jim Parrack), Jason Stackhouse's (Ryan Kwanten) best friend and most notable for punching implausibly above his weight with gorgeous young vampire Jessica (Deborah Ann Woll)—and having a ludicrously overbearing redneck mother (Dale Raoul). After Jessica and Jason start casually hooking up, Hoyt spends most of this season drifting between angry and depressed, then towards the end of the season he asks Jessica to 'glamour' him (old vampire mind-trick) to make him forget both her and Jason entirely. Asking the girl who loved him to wipe herself from his memory was a beautiful variation on wanting to take back our bad decisions but never being able to.

But beyond that, even the side-plots this season were lacking. Sometime short order cook Lafayette (Nelsan Ellis) starts the season bereft at the death of his lover Jesus (Kevin Alejandro), but after getting tortured by Jesus' grandpa has a quick chat to Jesus' ghost and is suddenly back to his bitchy best. (Obviously!) Iraqi war vet Terry (Todd Lowe) kills his commanding officer Patrick (Scott Foley) to save his family, and then a ghost sucks up the body and everything is just okay. There's a group of super-hating rednecks, but they mostly get killed, and with no effect on anyone we care about. Particularly disappointing was that all of the side-plots got resolved early on which, though it left the last few episodes clear for the main plot, meant that they all felt anti-climactic. We spent so much time with Terry for eight episodes and then his complicated shit is all just *over* and we move on to something else for the remaining four episodes of the season?

Which brings us to the last, perhaps most, perplexing decision of Season 5. As we all know, the show's creator Alan Ball is moving on at the end of this season. Typically, the chivalrous thing to do in these circumstances is to clear the decks and give the new crew a free run at the show. Instead, for the first time in the series so far, the main plot doesn't actually resolve at the end of the season. Bill drinks all of Lilith's[2] (Jessica Clark) sacred blood and then turns into something or other, we don't know what yet... and then the show is over.

All I can say is, I'm glad I'm not charged with coming in and making sense of all that in Season 6. That being said, I'll be back for the next season. Where else can you watch super-hot vampires killing almost indiscriminately and/or getting creatively naked with each other—or at least, not on pay-per-view?

– B. C. Roberts, 2012

[1] For those not in the know, Russell is the oldest and therefore strongest vampire in *True Blood*. A three thousand-year-old megalomaniac, Russell opposed "mainstreaming" (where vampires and humans live together) and killed a news anchor on TV to demonstrate the viciousness of vampires. He was supposed to have been killed by Bill and Eric but they buried him in concrete instead. And of course he escaped and that got everyone upset because having the most powerful psychopath in the world running around causing trouble is less than ideal.
[2] Lilith is the first vampire created by God before He created man. Which fails mostly to explain why people can be turned into vampires but not vice versa. But you know what religious fundamentalists are like. Just ask Paul Ryan about, well, anything really.

-:--:--:--:--:- *GS* -:--:--:--:--:-

COLLABORATION ENTRIES

Anticipating *Agents of S.H.I.E.L.D.*

It is hard to know precisely what to think about *Agents of SHIELD* (let's just be clear from the outset that I'm not typing it with full stops in between, and it will have to be really good to deserve a place in my text expander).

Despite all the hype, all the previews, even now reviews of the pilot (thanks IGN), the big open question is whether it is really possible to have an entire TV series based on a world of super heroes, without any super heroes. On the one hand I love the focus on [relatively] ordinary people who newly have to deal with a super-heroic world. This idea has obviously been done before, but I can't remember where or by whom. I'm sure Rachel will tell me. But I'm also sure that all of those books/comics/movies I can't remember didn't have to maintain interest over the length of time a successful TV show will be hoping to – though for Whedon, this only needs two full seasons to beat all of his recent efforts.

(Actually the one I can think of *Halo: ODST* which follows normal soldiers in a world where Master Chief and the Spartan soldiers can win entire wars on their own. I never played it despite being a massive *Halo* fan so maybe I'm not so taken with the premise after all.)

Anyway, the most important thing to remember about *Agents of SHIELD* is that it probably won't be very good and people probably won't notice.

– B. C. Roberts, 2013

-:--:--:--:--:- *GS* -:--:--:--:--:-

Geek Speak Magazine: Year One

B. C. Roberts
Contributing Writer
Nationality: Australian

Discovered *Geek Speak*: Through a friendship forged in trivia with the illustrious Editor.

Joined *Geek Speak*: Issue 1, March 2010

Because: I always hoped I would one day be cool enough to write for an e-zine.

First Piece: A review of *Underworld*.

Best Piece: It's a hard one because I'm normally critical of my work but I quite like my *Spider-Man* review.

Favorite Piece: I really love Rachel Day's defense of love stories in genre movies in the last issue; it almost made me change my mind. And I love Project Film Geek as a fellow tragic for bad movies (I'm the guy who loves *DOA*). Apart from that I'm just generally in awe of the people who write all the TV reviews.

***Geek Speak* Memories:** Far and away my favorite part of writing for *Geek Speak* is my correspondence with the Editor-in-Chief. Since I'm typically a week late with submissions, or otherwise disorganized, I love the chiding e-mails Rachel sends out. It makes me feel like one of her charges, the way that she manages to sound lovely with this threatening undertone. Exactly like Mary Poppins.

– B. C. Roberts, 2011

-:--:--:--:--:- *GS* -:--:--:--:--:-

Since We've Been Gone

You mean the world hasn't stopped turning without us?

October 24, 2011. That, friends, was the last time this magazine published an issue, our twentieth. Now, with our fancy-pants new makeover and our collective fire rekindled, we're finally back to gladden geek hearts the world over (none more than our own) with our thoughts on all things genre—but in the intervening six months, we have to concede that, well, stuff has happened. Important genre stuff, on which we have not yet had the chance to share our so-very-profound thoughts. So let us take a trip back, back into the past with a whirlwind tour of the notable genre occurrences that have passed us by, and see what our crack staff found exciting, disappointing and otherwise noteworthy since we've been gone...

B. C. Roberts
Contributing Writer

(The worst part about this feature is that I've had Kelly Clarkson stuck in my head for the last week.)

Genre Highlight: *Zone One* by Colson Whitehead is a clear standout. Well-reviewed by critics who downplay its genre, *Zone One* is a perceptive perspective on how contemporary America might deal with a zombie apocalypse – namely with public relations and corporate sponsorship.

Genre Lowlight: *Once Upon a Time* was hugely disappointing after a promising start, so that sucked. The final season of *Chuck* was truly awful and the ending would have left me angry if the show hadn't already burnt through every ounce of goodwill I had left for it. I also just read *The Hunger Games* trilogy (a bit late, I know) and would like to add to the chorus of what on earth was Collins thinking when she wrote *Mockingjay* or *Morninglark* or whatever it was. Holy crap that is a train wreck of a book. It's so bad that JK Rowling orgasms every time she thinks about it – it's the perfect proof of how much better she is.

Biggest Surprise: Undoubtedly the biggest surprise was that Bioware managed to fuck up the ending of *Mass Effect 3* so badly that fans called for a rewrite. They guys and girls at Bioware crafted an amazing game in which the entire universe shifts around your choices only to provide an ending where no choice you could make made any difference. The lack of understanding of what people actually liked about the game is just willfully stupid. Good work!!

Biggest Disappointment: Funny how some of my other sections were about disappointments already. There really is a lot of crap around. I'm going to go and watch a quality movie. Has anyone seen my copy of *Balls of Fury*?
(Hahaha, as if I have a physical copy of a movie.)

– B. C. Roberts, 2012

-:--:--:--:--:- *GS* -:--:--:--:--:-

Meet the Mutants: Beast and White Queen

With the hotly-anticipated X-Men: First Class in theaters this June, we take a look at the decidedly non-canonical line-up...

Prequels almost always suck. We know this. Nevertheless, there is something unbearably fascinating about them, something that makes us long for yet more back story, yet more insight into beloved characters and worlds, and yet more – almost inevitable – disappointment.

Just to give the uninitiated a little comic-y history, in the lead up to the film's June release (yes, it's a prequel, but of course we should all go see it) here we present the X-Class of 1962…

BEAST

Real Name: Dr Henry (Hank) McCoy
Created by: Stan Lee and Jack Kirby
First Appearance: *X-Men* #1, September 1963
Played by: Nicholas Hoult

Beast is one of the original X-Men and one of the few characters in this movie to actually be in the canonical first class at Xavier's School for Gifted Youngsters (the others being Jean Grey, Cyclops and Iceman). In each X-Men timeline, Beast starts off looking predominantly human with only oversized hands and feet to go with his super-strength and agility. He acquires his trademark blue fur and more animal-like features through medical experiments performed in some versions by Weapon X (the people Wolverine worked for) and in some versions by himself. He is the X-Men's scientific genius as well as being the most articulate and widely read.

Beast has spent most of his time working with the Avengers, rather than as part of the core X-Men team. He comes back to the X-Men whenever necessary and spends a good long time searching for a cure to the whatever it was that took all the mutants' powers away (well, it was a witch and I'm not sure how Beast thought he could find a cure to magic, but anyway).

His low-point is being played by Kelsey Grammer in *X3*, who captured the learned but not the action part of Beast's character. Hopefully his high point can come in this movie.

WHITE QUEEN

Real Name: Emma Grace Frost
Created by: Chris Claremont and John Byrne
First Appearance: *Uncanny X-Men* #129, January 1980.
Played by: January Jones

Emma Frost is a perplexing X-Men character. Taking the opposite trajectory to Magneto, Emma starts off as a villain and goes on to become absolutely central to the X-Men universe. By the current comics (or at least relatively recent – it's so hard to keep up) Emma is sleeping with Cyclops, and with Xavier incapacitated she's the top telepath. But she begins as a member of the Hellfire Club who, at least in one version, aim to bring back the Phoenix... killing Jean Grey in the process. But since Jean's not in this movie, it's hard to tell what their plan is for Emma this time out.

Apart from being a telepath, at some point along the line Emma survived a nuclear blast and, like Radioactive Man, got additional super powers – in her case the power to turn into diamond, making her indestructible. Of course, it's a special type of diamond which means she can still move just like a normal person, only more indestructiblier.

Emma also happens to be widely recognized as the most attractive comic book character out there. We're not sure if this is because she wears hardly any clothes, because she's a bit of a bitch, or because she has, like, crazy telepathic sex. Whatever it is, hopefully January Jones can do her justice.

– B. C. Roberts, 2011

To read the rest of this mutant introduction, see *The Best of Geek Speak Magazine, Vol. 1*, out now.

-:--:--:--:--:- *GS* -:--:--:--:--:-

Through the Pensieve: Thoughts on *Harry Potter*

B. C. Roberts
Staff-Writer
Australia
PRO

I came to the Harry Potter (or Harry Potty, as my two year-old insists on calling it) phenomenon earlier than some but later than many others. I first started reading the books some time after the fourth was released. I was twenty-one, in the latter stages of my time at university and had been afflicted with the usual type of winter cold. Faced with spending a week on the sofa in a time before bittorrent *[Not that we endorse such things – Ed.]* it seemed that a series of children's books would be the perfect way to get through it. The two people living with me at the time thought I was crazy, though both have since become converts – one almost immediately, though the other, *Geek Speak*'s Will Cashin, was more stubborn.

By this stage *HP* had already made the transition from kids' series to wider pop culture success, but it was still in the time before the first movie was released and it became part of the collective conscious. So my delightful then-girlfriend (now-wife) went out to the local bookstore and purchased a box set of the first four novels – unconvinced that this was an appropriate way for a grown man studying classical English literature to spend his time, but willing to indulge me in one of my less-crazy whims.

On the first day I read the first novel and immediately handed it back to her with the assurance that it was worth her valuable time (she was a diligent medical student and her time actually was valuable). I clearly remember opening the first book and then how quickly I was completely sold on the series. The opening chapter, as I'm sure most of you remember, is entitled "The Boy Who Lived," and it immediately won me over. Here was a main character famous for performing the simplest of acts in some extraordinary circumstances. A hero simply for doing what everyone else managed every day, and with no discernible special skills. At this point it was still many years before we learnt that Harry's survival was occasioned by a special type of magic or that there was anything fated about it. In those early days Harry was an unremarkable child who had merely failed to die when dying was expected of him.

I think the thing that drew me into *Harry Potter*, as it did so many others, was the masterful creation of a world in every way like our own but in which there lived, unseen and unsuspected, a whole community of superhumans. Because what are the wizards and witches of Harry's world but super? Their array of skills shames all but the most powerful superheroes: mastery of even a single of their skills would be sufficient to warrant inclusion on a team of superheroes; just think how many mutants become X-Men only being able to shoot fire, teleport, make themselves invisible, create force fields, heal by magic, or fly.

And simply the idea that one might, at the appropriate time in one's life, be removed from the quotidian to learn that one has hitherto undiscovered superpowers. Who hasn't wished they were special? Who hasn't been sure that there was more to them than those around them could see? For Harry, the moment Hagrid knocks down the door of that forsaken shack in the middle of nowhere, the dreams of every child who wished to be a hero are realized.

It is easy today to have become so accustomed to the wizarding world and the astounding feats of its inhabitants that we forget the extraordinary revelation at its heart: you, who do not fit into the world as you know it, are special beyond comprehension.

This revelation has long stood at the heart of fantasy literature but rarely has it been delivered with such poignancy and with such an understanding of the mundane nature of the contemporary world. Frodo is special, certainly, but predominantly owing to the ring given to him by his uncle, and his day-to-day world is completely unlike our own. Percy Jackson lives in the present but his importance derives from his parentage rather than his unwitting survival against evil. Perhaps the best example comes when Uncle Vernon is still trying to keep Harry as a Muggle and asks his nephew why Sunday might be his favorite day. "There's no post on Sunday," is Harry's dejected answer, before the wizarding world encroaches so spectacularly by delivering him hundreds of invitations to attend Hogwarts.

Needless to say I spent the remainder of my convalescence reading the four books consecutively, becoming more and more completely drawn into the world that Rowling creates so adeptly, and of course I was there on release day for the three that followed.

The Quote:

> *"You may not like him, Minister, but you can't deny: Dumbledore's got style."* – Kingsley Shacklebolt

– B. C. Roberts, 2011

For more of our collective ruminations on all things Potter, see *Geek Speak Magazine Presents: Through the Pensieve – Random Thoughts on Harry Potter and the Wizarding World,* out now.

-:--:--:--:--:- *GS* -:--:--:--:--:-

What We're Reading

All the Birds in the Sky by Charlie Jane Anders

This book is a blend of science fiction and fantasy with one of the two main characters being a witch and the other a futuristic scientist. Where Patricia (the witch) communes with birds and turns evil-doers into turtles, Laurence (the scientist) builds time machines, AI and dimensional portals. The story really hinges on the relationship between these two characters who meet in school, lose each other for a while and then later find each other again. Their connection seems tenuous at times – they spend much less time together than they spend with the other formative magic-y / science-y people in their lives and yet it is their bond which is depicted as being the strongest. I quite liked the book while I was reading it, but I finished it a few days ago and just had to look up what the characters names were, so I don't think it's a particularly lasting read. Fun for the time but not one that will stay with you.

– B. C. Roberts, Columnist Plenipotentiary

All the Birds in the Sky by Charlie Jane Anders
Science Fiction/Urban Fantasy/Apocalypse | Tor Books | 2016

-:--:--:--:--:- *GS* -:--:--:--:--:-

Company Town by Madeline Ashby

The book follows Hwa, a bodyguard for sex workers living on an offshore oil rig in Newfoundland. The scene is semi-dystopic – it's set in a high-tech future where opportunities to live outside the control of large corporations are rare – but the depiction of sex work as employment imbued with dignity is commendable.

This is a standalone novel so it rockets through the main plot with little distraction. There are no torturous love interests in this one. The pace mostly even makes up for some thin characterization, especially Hwa's new boss, company man Daniel. A lot hinges on his motivations being believable but it feels like after spending so much time creating an emotionally defensive Korean taekwondo teaching bodyguard that there was no room left for any other complex characters.

Still, overall a solid B-grade read.

– B. C. Roberts, Columnist Plenipotentiary

Company Town by Madeleine Ashby
SF Dystopia | Tor Books | 2016

Library of Souls by Ransom Riggs

I have just this minute finished this third book in the *Miss Peregrine's Home for Peculiar Children* trilogy. Which was thankfully a trilogy because I started the first book yesterday thinking it was a standalone, and halfway through began to worry that everything wouldn't be resolved. At least the trilogy is complete, and I was not left midway through an unfinished series where I had to wait some awful amount of time for a resolution. I hate that.

The trilogy is great but nothing at all what I expected. From the 'Now a Major Motion Picture' and the promotional poster of Eva Green as a beautiful Miss Peregrine, I thought I was going to be reading something more *Harry Potter* and less *Pride and Prejudice and Zombies*-meets-*The Hunger Games*.

I am often late to the party on these things, but I have read way, way too many of the modern Young Adult three-volume novel and I wasn't really looking for another one. Somewhere throughout the journey from *The Hunger Games* to *Divergent* to *Shatter Me* (I'm actually ashamed of that one), I became aware that at some point along the line, teenagers saving the world in three acts became a genre unto-itself.

SPOILER ALERT. This trilogy bucks convention and provides a comprehensively happy ending. As in, the protagonist teenage lovers both save the world, and don't die doing it, and don't lose any close family members (like little sisters) and they still end up together at the end. After all the death and love triangles of the others in the genre, it's a nice change.

– B. C. Roberts, Columnist Plenipotentiary

Library of Souls (Peculiar Children #3) by Ransom Riggs
YA | Quirk Books | 2015

You, Too, Can Save the World – Our Crack Staff Reflects on the Ultimate Everyman

B. C. Roberts
Contributing Writer
Australia
NEUTRAL

There is something irresistibly attractive about Batman. He is the black sheep of the superhero world. The guy who doesn't trust any of the other supers and has a plan for taking out each one of them should they turn rogue. I always wondered: what would happen if Batman turned bad? Could he take down all the others with his sneaky plans?

Probably not. Because, you know, Batman, for all his wiles, doesn't actually have any powers at all. This being the case he is, in fact, the least plausible hero out there – yes, even less plausible than a guy being hit by radiation and gaining the power of [insert the power of pretty much every superhero except Superman].

With Batman we are being asked to believe that one rich guy with a cape could triumph over the all-powerful Superman whenever he feels like it just because he has a kryptonite ring. That it is more likely that he would land even one punch on the Man of Steel, rather than Superman simply eye-lasering him from outer-space. Sure.

Now, the Nolan Batman movies are undoubtedly improvements over the awful campy movies preceding them and *Batman Begins*, in particular, is a lesson in how to do an origin story. But Nolan (unlike in *Inception*) doesn't appear to trust his audience to put together the symbolism of his work, insisting instead on beating us over the head with the fact that Batman is the dark knight and Harvey Dent is the white knight, etc. etc. My God, was there anyone by the end of that second movie who hadn't figured out that Batman was a symbol of the anti-hero? Jesus Christ, he beats the crap out of nameless thugs like they insulted Wayne Manor's opulent décor.

In the end, Batman stands as the Harry Potter of a bygone age: the guy anyone could be. Except the kids who believed that then were just as stupid as the ones who believe a Mattel wand will make their cat fly now.

– *B. C. Roberts, 2012*

-:--:--:--:--:- *GS* -:--:--:--:--:-

ABOUT THE AUTHOR

Disfigured in a factory accident that warped his brain but expanded his mind, **B. C. Roberts** has chosen to use his talents to dissect the highs and lows of popular culture. Never short of an opinion or a cranium-splitting headache, he can always be relied upon to fight the twin evils of stupidity and ignorance wherever they arise. He lives in your darkest fears.

Also from Overlord Publishing

Buffy the Vampire Slayer, Season Eight: Reviewed
Geek Speak Magazine Presents: The Best of Amy Sharma
Geek Speak Magazine Presents: The Best of B. C. Roberts
Geek Speak Magazine Presents: The Best of David Baldwin
Geek Speak Magazine Presents: The Best of Geonn Cannon
Geek Speak Magazine Presents: The Best of Jason Luna
Geek Speak Magazine Presents: The Best of Jason Murdoch
Geek Speak Magazine Presents: The Best of K. Burtt
Geek Speak Magazine Presents: The Best of Kate Nagy
Geek Speak Magazine Presents: The Best of Kellie Sheridan
Geek Speak Magazine Presents: The Best of Kim Sorensen
Geek Speak Magazine Presents: The Best of Mark Ritchie
Geek Speak Magazine Presents: The Best of Rachel Day
Geek Speak Magazine Presents: The Best of Rachel Hyland
Geek Speak Magazine Presents: The Best of Sara Paige
Geek Versus Geek
The Grand Tour: A Georgette Heyer Travel Guide
Project Film Geek: 1929
Reading Heyer: The Black Moth
Reading Heyer: Powder and Patch
Through the Pensieve – Random Thoughts on Harry Potter
The Top 13
Undercovers: Reviewed
Under the Dome: Reviewed
The White Queen: Reviewed
YA Novels: Reviewed

www.ingramcontent.com/pod-product-compliance
Lightning Source LLC
Chambersburg PA
CBHW031626040426
42452CB00007B/695

* 9 7 8 1 9 2 5 7 7 0 1 8 6 *